DRUG-PROOF YOUR KIDS

Other books by Stephen Arterburn

Hooked on Life: How to Totally Recover from Addiction and Codependency
(co-author Tim Timmons) (Oliver-Nelson)
Growing Up Addicted (Ballantine)
How Will I Tell My Mother? (co-author Jerry Arterburn) (Oliver-Nelson)
When Someone You Love Is Someone You Hate (co-author David Stoop) (Word, Inc.)

Other books by Jim Burns

Handling Your Hormones: The Straight Scoop on Love and Sexuality
(Harvest House)
The Youth Builder: Today's Resource for Relational Youth Ministry
(Harvest House)
Getting in Touch with God (Harvest House)
The Youth Worker Book of Case Studies (Gospel Light)
High School Ministry (co-author Mike Yaconelli) (Zondervan Publishing)
Growth Unlimited (Harvest House)
Life of Christ Series (Harvest House)
The Incredible Christ
Greatest Story Ever Told
Getting Your Priorities Straight
Radical for the King
Leader's Guide
Christian Growth Series (Harvest House)
Commitment to Growth
Building Relationships. . .With God and Others
Congratulations, You Are Gifted
Leader's Guide
Christian Life Series (Harvest House)
Putting God First
Making Your Life Count
Living Your Life. . .As God Intended
Giving Yourself to God
Leader's Guide

DRUG-PROOF YOUR KIDS

A PREVENTION GUIDE & AN INTERVENTION PLAN

STEPHEN ARTERBURN & JIM BURNS

PUBLISHING

Pomona, California

DRUG-PROOF YOUR KIDS
Copyright © 1989 by Focus on the Family

Library of Congress Cataloging-in-Publication Data

Arterburn, Stephen, 1953-
  Drug-proof your kids / Stephen Arterburn and Jim Burns.
  p.   cm.
  ISBN 0-929608-26-7 : $7.99
  1. Teenagers—United States—Drug use.   2. Teenagers—United
States—Alcohol use.   3. Drug abuse—United States—Prevention.
4. Alcoholism—United States—Prevention.   5. Child rearing—United
States.   I. Burns, Jim, 1953-   . II. Title.
HV5824.Y68A78 1989
649'.4—dc20   89-17245
                                                            CIP

Published by Focus on the Family Publishing, Pomona, CA 91799.
Distributed by Word, Inc., Dallas, Texas.

Unless otherwise noted, Scripture quotations are from The Holy Bible: New International
Version. Copyright 1973, 1978, 1984 by the International Bible Society.

"Frequently-Seen Stages in Adolescent Chemical Use" Chart. © Dennis Nelson,
CompCare Publishers, Minneapolis. Used by permission.

Designer: Sherry Nicolai Russell
Black and White Photographer: Ron Smith
Color Photographer: The Stock Market/Henley & Savage
Printed in the United States of America

89 90 91 92 93 94 / 10 9 8 7 6 5 4 3 2 1

With love and gratitude to Sandy and Cathy.
This book, our ministry and our message would be incomplete
without your loving and sacrificial belief in us.
Your lives are an intricate part of this project.

Contents

Acknowledgments

Special thanks to Katie Temple and Karen Walters for always going the second and even the third mile with such joyful spirits. We are blessed to have you as our co-workers.

We also wish to express our deepest gratitude and respect for the wonderful ministry of Focus on the Family. Janet Kobobel is not only a talented editor but also a wonderful person. Thank you, Janet, for your invaluable help. Thank you, Peb Jackson, for your commitment to serve the body of Christ. You are an inspiration.

Preface

We wish we didn't have to write this book. We wish that not one child had to deal with the incredible pressure to try drugs and alcohol. Unfortunately, the overwhelming majority of kids you know and love will experiment with these substances. Worse yet, many of these kids and their families will suffer greatly from addiction and the other traumas that go along with substance abuse.

Far too many parents *assume* the monumental problem of drug abuse will never touch their children. Yet our experience tells us that no one is safe. We've seen thousands of kids—rich, poor, Christian, non-Christian, tall, short, high IQ, learning-disabled, college graduates, fourth-graders—seduced into drug and alcohol abuse. We've seen wonderful families blown apart and caught totally by surprise when drugs and alcohol become an intimate and awful reality in their family.

This book contains a drug-proof plan we know works. A desperate mother came to us recently and said, "If I follow this plan, will you guarantee my children will be drug-free?" We can't guarantee that every parent who reads this book will never see his or her children struggle with substance abuse. We can say that if parents follow the steps of this drug-proof plan, thousands of children will be spared the anguish of drug abuse. And while that's no guarantee, it's the best prevention measure you can take.

CHAPTER ONE

Drugs at Your Doorstep

Listen to Terry, age sixteen: "I don't think it even entered my parents' minds that I was a teenage alcoholic. After all, I was active in my church youth group. My Christian faith was extremely visible at school. I got good grades, and my choice of friends was better than most. I came from a good Christian family, and everything looked great on the outside. They didn't suspect that almost every day for the past two years, I was getting high. It's really kind of funny how you can be so deceptive to your own parents. I wanted their help, but I figured they wouldn't know what to say or do."

Is Terry's story unusual? Hardly. Even the best of kids get entangled with drug and alcohol addiction, and their parents often have no idea. In fact, a majority of young people will experiment with drugs or alcohol, and the statistics don't show much difference between churched and unchurched kids.[1] When it comes to heavy use (using a substance six or more times within a month), the figures for the two groups are almost the same.

Darlene is fourteen years old. She's an above-average student, very pretty, well-liked by her peers, faithful in attending church, and comes from a stable, middle-class home. Everyone believes Darlene has a lot going for her. By the time she graduates from high school, however, the chances are (estimating conservatively):

- 85 percent she will experiment with alcohol.
- 57 percent she will try an illicit drug.
- 33 percent she will smoke marijuana on occasion.
- 33 percent she will get drunk at least once a month.
- 25 percent she will smoke marijuana regularly.
- 17 percent she will try cocaine or crack.[2]

The young people from whom these statistics are derived have names and faces. They come from every walk of life: rich and poor; liberal and conservative; Christian, Jewish, and Hindu; rural, suburban, and inner city. In twentieth-century America, we have a growing drug problem from which no one is immune.

Every parent wants to believe his or her children will escape the epidemic of drug abuse and alcoholism that is daily engulfing thousands of young people. Unfortunately, no matter where you live, your children have not escaped. You probably have hoped you would be able to do and say the right things to make them immune to temptation. You may have prayed, begged, and threatened in your attempts to keep the epidemic from touching your family. Yet we've heard what seems like thousands of anguished parents tell us, "We never dreamed it would happen to us."

Every child is susceptible to what most authorities today are calling "Drugs: Public Enemy #1."

The substances and form change rapidly, but our drug problem remains and has even intensified in recent years. Today the problem is so desperate that gangs kill each other for the right to distribute drugs to your children. Elementary school playgrounds are infiltrated with kids who earn money by turning on the most innocent among us to "magic pills to make you happy." No sector of our society has escaped. Whatever your walk of life, wherever your neighborhood, drugs are at your doorstep.

Larry was in my (Jim's) youth group at church. He was a fun-loving kid, and everybody liked him. But one day his parents sat in my office deeply grieving the loss of their only son. The night before, Larry went to a party, got drunk, and lost control of his car while speeding down a busy highway. Three kids were dead, and the driver of the other car was in critical condition. Apparently Larry was a teenage alcoholic. None of us ever knew until it was too late.

His parents kept shaking their heads as we planned the funeral, saying, "We had no idea. We just assumed it would never happen to people like us. We suspected Larry drank periodically, but we thought it was harmless. Please tell other Christian parents—before it's too late—that their kids aren't safe just because they're involved in church activities."

The actions taken to curb this mounting epidemic can be summed up as too little, too late. Neither the government nor the private sector has done enough to reduce demand for drugs or to get them out of our schools, our neighborhoods, our communities, our country. Each day the epidemic robs us of lives that would otherwise make a difference in this world. People who could run new companies, invent useful products, and care for the needy are destroyed daily. With the push of a needle, a snort up the nose, or a wild drive by an intoxicated kid, drugs steal our nation's future.

We are the most violent, crime-ridden country in the industrial world. This is partly because we are the biggest user of illegal drugs; we have 5 percent of the world's population and use 50 percent of the world's annual output of cocaine.[3] And while our future shoots up, snorts, and overdoses, various committees, bureaucracies, and misguided people, who are off on a quick-fix tangent, cripple the efforts needed to free our kids.

Why Too Little, Too Late?

In the 1988 presidential campaign, for the first time, both party platforms identified drug abuse as the nation's biggest problem. Yet the government has not produced the results parents need, and it may never be able to cut off completely the supply of drugs. Even as governmental resolve and force increase, so do the resolve and force of those who profit from our children's addictions. No matter how hard we fight as a nation, those who run the drug trade will find a way to expand their markets and increase their profits. No, the government will not solve this problem.

However, we believe together we can drug-proof our young people. That hope lies in parents who will take action—one family, one neighborhood, one community at a time. Pointing fingers at the state capital or Washington, D.C., won't get the job done. Each parent must step back and answer the question, "What can I do to save the children?"

Too few parents ever ask that question. Fewer still take action. Let's look at four major reasons parents are not making the difference they could in this epidemic:

1. *Ignorance.* Even in the midst of massive publicity about this problem, many people don't believe that drugs and alcohol are threats to their children. They read the paper and watch the television news, but somehow they rationalize that the stories are about faraway people in faraway places. They don't realize that no neighborhood has been left unscathed by this problem. As a result, when their own children get

into trouble, they're the last to figure it out.

We spend a great deal of our time training Christian workers to deal more effectively with youth and families, and we're always amazed at the ignorance found even among the clergy. In a recent study of the church and substance abuse, 92 percent of the pastors surveyed said drug abuse is a major problem among young people in their communities. However, when asked if there's a serious problem in their own churches, only 13 percent said yes. Yet the same study showed only a slight difference between churched and unchurched youth when it comes to usage of drugs and alcohol.

DRUG USE AMONG TEENS[4]

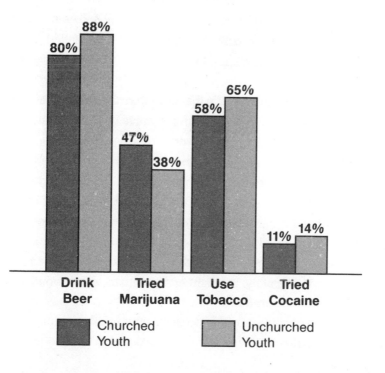

A while back, I (Steve) counseled a parent whose teenager was a full-blown alcoholic, a victim of the epidemic of abuse of the oldest known drug. The girl's symptoms were clear, but her parents were totally ignorant of her condition, unaware she even drank.

I became involved through a call from her youth pastor. She was in his office, and he didn't know what to do with her. When I arrived, it was apparent many tears had been shed that day. This beautiful young girl and her youth pastor helped me understand the nature of the problem. By the time he had picked her up that morning, she had consumed a pint of whiskey and half of a fifth of vodka.

A girl of about 110 pounds consuming so much alcohol had a tolerance far surpassing that of most drinkers of the same weight. I asked if her friends had ever mentioned that her drinking was different from theirs. She admitted that on several occasions, her friends had expressed deep concern about her drinking. They had pointed out that when they consumed a couple of drinks, she consumed an entire bottle. When they got drunk on three or four drinks, she was hardly affected.

Tolerance plays a large role in the development of alcohol addiction; most people must be able to drink a great deal of alcohol to get addicted to it. This girl had a severe drinking problem that needed treatment. Hers was not a mild case or an example of an adolescent attempting to adjust to life. This was true addiction to a chemical.

The parents were blissfully unaware of the problem. They were Christians but so uninvolved in her life that they hadn't noticed she drank and had failed to see her progression into addiction. Their ignorance had left their daughter to fight her way out of the problem on her own. Fortunately, her fight ended with a call to a youth pastor. Others are not so fortunate.

2. *Denial.* It's always easier to deny than to take action—at least initially. Denial takes many forms, but it's always used to avoid pain

or delay action. We tend to be lazy; our nature is to put off until tomorrow what needs to be dealt with today. So we repress or ignore what's in front of us.

We refuse to notice when our children develop a pattern of weekend illnesses that are manifestations of being hung over. We turn away at the sight of dilated pupils or drooping eyelids, excusing them as signs of a mere lack of rest.

Some parents know about the use of drugs and alcohol by their children but deny the seriousness of the problem. While the children form lifetime patterns of dependent behavior, the parents rationalize that what they see is a stage or a phase their kids will outgrow.

Parents in denial refuse to face their children's condition because they're unwilling to experience the temporary pain that comes when you intervene in a person's life. Denial blocks out the need to act, allowing the drug problem to grow, the young addict to suffer, and the family to descend into dishonesty and farce, where everyone learns how *not* to deal with problems.

Another major concern leading to denial is the stigma that addiction brings to a family. The embarrassment of other people knowing that all is not well prevents parents from taking action. Saving the family's image is more important than doing what needs to be done.

Denial is deadly, however, and must be overcome. The stigma of a drug problem in the family is never as great as the pain of a death due to drug overdose or some other drug-related incident.

Are Christian parents immune from denial? Absolutely not. Because of a distorted view of spirituality, many Christian parents simply refuse to believe their kids might be involved in drugs or alcohol. They think their faith somehow insures the plague cannot contaminate their children. But no one is exempt.

3. *Guilt.* Parents often are unable to act because they blame themselves for their children's condition. They play the "if only"

game and always lose. Berating their methods of child rearing, they take on the weight of every poor decision made by their kids. They're unable to make tough, necessary decisions because they're paralyzed by guilt and remorse.

Wrapped up in their own problems, these parents don't see a clear path for their children, so they do what's easy. They encourage the kids to do better rather than demand the end of drug and alcohol use. Some parents allow their children to drink alcohol at home under the permissive battle cry, "If my child is going to do it, I prefer it be done under my roof." This dysfunctional philosophy comes from trying to compensate for past mistakes.

Guilt, the great paralyzer, stands in the way of rational thinking and parenting actions that produce change. It's a key reason we do too little, too late. Only when parents become aware that guilt sometimes keeps them from making the right decisions can they be free to help their children and not place undeserved blame on themselves.

4. *Fear.* My (Jim's) friend Sylvia's first marriage ended in a tragedy, and her second marriage was a tragedy from the beginning. Her new husband was in the later stages of alcoholism and was violent and abusive. Sylvia became a textbook victim, and her children turned to experimenting with drugs and alcohol. She knew about her kids' problems but was afraid to confront them because, as she told me one afternoon, "If they also reject me, I have nothing left to live for."

Many parents, like Sylvia, don't react appropriately to drugs at their doorstep because they fear their children will reject them forever. Some fear what might lie ahead if their kids do change—the fear of the unknown. Others are afraid of doing the wrong thing and making the problem worse.

Each fear becomes another excuse not to act, allowing the drug epidemic to continue. If kids are going to stop abusing chemicals, parents must move beyond their fears and into action.

We have to learn what's helpful and then do it. Ignorance, denial, guilt, and fear must be overcome by a tough kind of love. This is how you begin to drug-proof your kids and stop the growing epidemic.

To succeed, we need an effective plan of attack. And any such plan has to start with a clear understanding of just how bad the problem is today. We'll look at that next.

CHAPTER TWO

Just How Bad Is It?

A frantic mother called to tell me (Steve) she had found some suspicious things in her daughter's room. She didn't know what to do. I told her to bring the items to my office; she arrived about an hour later.

Her hands shook as she laid each item on my desk. There was a small, brown vial. It was empty. There was half a capsule, also empty. Then there was a syringe and a rubber tube. The final item was a glass pipe with some water drops condensed on the inside of its small globe.

The mother knew what lay before her: proof that her daughter was a drug abuser. She wept as she told of the times she had found other items that were all explained away by her daughter—a joint that "was placed in her pocket by mistake"; a pill "she was just keeping for a friend with a cold." This mother felt guilty for not seeking help sooner, for denying it could happen to her child.

As this woman learned so painfully and personally, society has become a victim of drug abuse and alcoholism in a way never seen before. And the problem continues to grow. Every day we hear of the largest drug bust in history, of another life wasted by drunk driving, or of a newborn baby addicted to cocaine.

Talk to your children, and if they're open, they'll tell you of kids who peddle new drug products out of school lockers or on neighborhood corners; of the kids who have started smoking cigarettes, moved on to marijuana, and then into inhaling the fumes from burning pieces of crack cocaine; of a society of kids who drink to get drunk with increasing frequency.

The staggering scope of our society's drug and alcohol problem begins to take shape in the following statistics:

Every day in America, police arrest 500 busloads of people, and of those, 70 percent, or 350 busloads, have an illegal drug in their system at the time of arrest.

Every day in America, Americans snort a bathtub full of cocaine: 325 pounds. Even sadder, every day 5,000 people try cocaine for the first time.

Every day in America, Americans smoke 85,000 pounds of marijuana. That's a bale of marijuana the size of a small house.

Every day in America, Americans consume 15.7 million gallons of beer and ale. That's 28 million six-packs of beer, enough cans to fill a baseball stadium thirty feet deep.

Every day in America, Americans drift off to sleep with the help of six dump trucks full of sleeping pills—30 million tablets every single night. (And Valium is outselling aspirin!)

Every day in America, Americans consume 1.2 million gallons of hard liquor, enough to get 26 million people thoroughly drunk.[1]

The toll that alcohol alone has taken on this country is staggering. According to the National Council on Alcoholism, alcohol has been a problem for 56 million families, costing an annual $116 billion.[2] The American Hospital Association reports that half of hospital admissions are alcohol related.

As staggering as the numbers are, they don't calculate the suffering endured by those who are raised in an alcoholic home or are maimed by a drunken driver, or who lose everything due to an alcohol problem. The answer to the question "How bad is it?" is simple. It is very bad.

How bad is the problem as it relates specifically to young people? The National Council on Alcoholism offers the following statistics:

- The first drinking experience today usually occurs around age twelve, in contrast to ages thirteen to fourteen in the 1940s and '50s. It is no longer unusual for twelve- or even ten-year-olds to have serious alcohol abuse problems.
- Since 1966, the number of high school students who are intoxicated at least once a month has more than doubled.
- In one public school survey of 27,000 kids, 11 percent reported they were hooked on alcohol.
- By the ninth grade, 56 percent have tried alcohol. By the senior year, more than nine out of ten have taken their first drink.
- Alcohol-related highway deaths are the number-one killer of fifteen- to twenty-four-year-olds.
- An estimated 3.3 million drinkers ages fourteen to seventeen are showing signs they may develop serious alcohol-related problems.[3]

In 1987, Secretary of Health and Human Services Otis Bowen said nearly 5 million adolescents have drinking problems, or three of every ten. He complained that brewers and beer distributors are spending $15-20 million a year to market their products to college campuses, encouraging heavy drinking, which contributes to poor grades, vandalism, injuries, and death.[4]

Kids today are making decisions about alcohol and drugs when they are twelve to fourteen, whereas in the preceding generation they made those decisions at ages sixteen to eighteen. The younger a person starts drinking, the more likely he or she is to develop alcohol-related problems later in life.

U.S. News & World Report presented its own evidence of the growing epidemic, coming up with different numbers but the same basic message. They reported that:

- two of every three high school seniors have drunk alcohol within the past month.
- 5 percent drink daily.
- 40 percent of sixth graders have tasted wine coolers.
- by age eighteen, a child will have seen 100,000 beer commercials.[5]

According to *Newsweek* magazine, when teenagers were asked what was the biggest problem facing them, 66 percent agreed it was alcohol and drugs.[6]

Since the mid-1980s, the addition of crack cocaine has fueled our nation's drug problem beyond any level anyone could have imagined. Cocaine was previously the drug of the rich and famous, but in the form of crack, it's cheap and available to the masses. Here are some of the facts and stories surrounding the crack epidemic:

- As of June 1985, the New York City police had not made a single crack arrest. In the first ten months of 1988, they made 19,074.[7]
- In Los Angeles, gangs functioning as armed crack distributors were responsible for 387 murders in 1987.[8]
- In Atlanta, cocaine overdose deaths were up more than 250 percent between 1986 and 1987.[9]
- In Philadelphia, cocaine deaths increased 259 percent between

the first and fourth quarters of 1987.[10]
- In San Francisco, cocaine deaths increased by 213 percent from the first half of 1986 to the first half of 1987.[11]
- In Detroit, a Little League team folded because the kids were too busy selling crack to play baseball.[12]
- Some schools have had to ban students from carrying pagers to restrict the sale of drugs.[13]
- Big cities aren't the only ones affected. Colorado State University in Fort Collins surveyed 1,472 seniors from 24 rural high schools in 7 states. Crack was found in all but one of the schools. The study concluded that crack is available almost anywhere in the United States.
- In 1985, a jumbo vial of crack cost $40. Today that price has dropped to less than $15 in most places, making the drug more affordable than ever.[14]

Why Is the Problem Getting Worse?

What accounts for the steady worsening of the problem? For one thing, take a look at the millions of dollars the liquor industry spends to bombard us with those thousands of messages to drink—and drink often—to be "with it" and accepted. Kids watching those commercials want nothing more than to be accepted. *The Bottom Line on Alcohol in Society* recently presented a summary of the strategy of the liquor industry:

1. Increase the number of occasions on which current drinkers consume alcohol. The goal is to raise the number of times during the day when people drink, the number of days when they drink, and the number of occasions on which drinking is the thing to do.

2. Increase the percentage of those who drink. In other words, turn the 90 percent of high school students who have experimented with

alcohol into regular users.

3. Position alcoholic beverages to compete with soft drinks as "thirst quenchers" and "refreshment beverages." Evidence of this strategy includes the sponsoring of marathons and other running events, along with the development and marketing of wine coolers.[15]

The number of sixth graders who have tried alcohol today has increased by almost 150 percent compared to six years ago.[16] We believe one of the major reasons is the slick marketing of wine coolers. When fourth graders were asked about the pressure to drink, one in three said that even at their age they experienced tremendous pressure to drink wine coolers. One in four had succumbed to the pressure, and by the sixth grade, 40 percent of the kids had consumed wine coolers.[17]

The disguising of this product as something healthful, with real fruit juice, and its presentation as part of the life-style of those who have it all together, make the wine cooler the perfect entry product into drinking. The Kool-Aid of this generation is hooking our youngsters earlier into the addiction process and, because of children's fragile, developing bodies, locking them into that process more deeply and quickly than ever.

Behind the increasing numbers regarding crack and other illegal drugs is a strong economic force that is difficult to counter. Every gang member, every high school dropout selling drugs, and every pusher on every street corner is part of an industry propelled by a network of drug cartels based mainly in Colombia. These are sophisticated, well-organized, violent underworld syndicates with vast experience in drug trafficking. Their goal is to expand their markets and increase their profits at all costs, and they have plenty of money to invest in the development of their business. The statistics show these organizations are achieving their goals—at the cost of our families and our nation's future.

A study of 700 teenagers over a period of eight years revealed that heavy drug use leads directly to many problems. Young drug users divorce more quickly, suffer from greater job instability, commit more serious crimes, and are generally more unhappy with their lives and relationships than others.[18] A generation of kids who are set up to fail in their personal and professional lives is a problem that parents must recognize and face.

We must be the transitional generation. Our kids are beginning to recognize how serious the problem is; we must act to help them solve it. This isn't just a faddish project or charity. It's a deeply needed movement that must be headed by caring parents. The problem isn't getting better, and we must not wait for someone else to solve it for us. We must act one person at a time to drug-proof our children.

The Drug-Proof Concept

Fortunately, there's good news. We can drug-proof our kids and save them from the pressure to use drugs or take the steps to stop using them. The idea is comparable to weatherproofing a home. You cannot do away with the weather. The storms and floods will come. But the wise person has prepared his or her home to withstand the forces of nature and not be destroyed. Likewise, drugs are there. Alcohol is always available. But the drug-proof child will not be destroyed by them.

At the end of the Sermon on the Mount in Matthew 7:24-27, Jesus told the following parable:

Therefore everyone who hears these words of mine and puts them into practice is like a wise man who built his house on the rock. The rain came down, the streams rose, and the winds blew and beat against that house; yet it did not fall, because it had its foundation on the rock. But everyone who hears these words of mine and does not put them into practice is like a foolish man who built his house on sand. The rain came down, the streams rose, and the winds blew and beat against that house, and it fell with a great crash.

Rain, wind, and storms will come to all our lives, but the wise family builds its foundation on the rock. Only the foolish assume sand is a strong enough foundation to hold against the storms of substance abuse in our world today.

Drug-proof kids are given the chance to become whole, healthy, strong, and free human beings. Their parents lay the foundation for them to flourish. But it isn't easy. It takes great determination and a commitment of study, time, finances, and prayer. It requires following a plan through every stage of a child's life.

I (Steve) work with a man who had two sons go through a drug treatment program. He determined his boys were in trouble, and he sought the best available help. He and his wife became deeply involved in the treatment process and were active in the long-term plan for recovery. He told me of their first Christmas together when both kids were off drugs and into recovery. He said it was the first time he felt like a truly free person, no longer a captive in his own house. The eggshells they had walked on over the past years were swept out the door.

Drug-proofing can begin at any age. Kids about to enter kindergarten need to be prepared for people who have stooped so low as to pass off drugs as "magic pills" to small children. (My [Jim's] five-year-old daughter is learning to say, "Hugs, not drugs.") If a child has already experimented with drugs, it's still not too late. Even if a child is grown, has a family, and is a practicing alcoholic, a parent can act to free the child from addiction. It's never too late to become involved with a person abusing drugs. There is always hope.

The key ingredient to a drug-proof plan is parents taking responsibility to help their children change. This duty cannot be delegated—

not to the school, church, or anyone else. Besides, no one else has a parent's power to motivate a child to change. Drug-proof kids have hope mainly because their parents have made a conscious decision to get involved.

Once you have accepted the responsibility to help your children, you are ready to form a plan and carry it out. Children involved with drugs and alcohol do not just wake up one day and decide to stop. They need all the help they can get, especially in the form of positive pressure from parents to change.

Let's face it: most kids will either think they're immune, or they will exercise the experimental nature of adolescence and play with fire. But if you design and implement a comprehensive plan, there's an excellent chance the children you love will be spared the destruction of drugs.

There are no shortcuts, no easy answers. We base our plan and this book on three principles.

1. God cares about families. The Bible shows God's concern for families and spells out His principles for parenting. These set the standard for families to resist drugs and raise fulfilled and successful children.

2. Common sense, genuine love, and communication make a long-term difference. Train a child in the way he should go, and when he is old he will not turn from it (Prov. 22:6). Common sense tells us such training requires a plan. An important ingredient of the plan is strong communication with our children, motivated by a deep sense of love and concern.

3. Always use the most effective drug and alcohol education, prevention, and treatment methods. We've included in this drug-proof plan only the best methods available. Sometimes people don't seek help simply because they don't know where to go or what to do. Some have received critical misinformation. We encourage you to

investigate all you can about "public enemy #1."

The drug-proof plan involves the following areas:

1. Education. Parents must obtain the knowledge they need about drugs, alcohol, and addiction. Then the information must be passed along to their kids. Unfortunately, this part of the plan is often neglected when parents assume their children already have the right information. Parents who gamble on others doing the educating while they remain silent are asking for trouble.

2. Prevention. Prevention involves rewards for responsible behavior and restrictions following irresponsible behavior. This is part of a good, overall parenting strategy that encourages kids to make right decisions and immediately feel the consequences of poor choices.

3. Identification. When parents become aware their children are using drugs or alcohol, they must immediately identify and evaluate the problem. There should be no such thing as "secret behavior." In this part of the plan, kids are not left to develop the problem on their own or figure out how to get out of it by themselves. It's a family problem. If it's happening in the family, it must be known and dealt with by everyone. A part of the identification process is evaluation of children's behavior so that if intervention is needed, it can be instituted as soon as possible.

4. Intervention. If the problem develops and is identified, this part of the plan allows for fast, appropriate parental action to extinguish the undesirable behavior.

5. Treatment. Treatment comes in many forms, but there is no substitute if it's needed. An important part of the plan is knowing what treatment resources are available and how to use them.

6. Supportive Follow-up. This could also be called "relapse prevention." It enables the family to be part of the ongoing recovery process rather than to unknowingly destroy the foundations of lifetime sobriety. The entire family must be involved.

7. Self-Evaluation. Parents can't intervene effectively in the lives of their children unless they have made some positive decisions regarding their own involvement with alcohol and drugs. You may need to begin a recovery program yourself. Evaluation is also important for those who were raised in the home of a substance-abusing parent or who live with a substance-abusing spouse. A great deal of help is available for adult children of alcoholics.

The plan is simple, comprehensive, and attainable if you're committed to saving your children. It's the best chance that you and your family will escape the heartache of addiction.

The drug-proof plan is *not* based on three key points. First, it is not based on quick fixes. Like the heroin addict who must shoot up for a fast fix, our "instant soup, push-button mentality" always looks for the fast and easy way out. This is one problem you can't put in a microwave for three minutes and be done with it. It takes time and effort. Quick fixes produce only quick failures.

Second, the plan is not based on new tricks. People are always trying to provide a one-dimensional answer for this multidimensional problem. Almost every day, someone arrives on the scene with a new cure-all. But it soon fails, because no one approach works. Beating drugs takes the coordination of several approaches and the cooperation of an entire community. Rather than new tricks, this problem requires old wisdom.

Third, the drug-proof plan is not based on the idea of "Let's wait for a miracle." Doing nothing is irresponsible. Too many helpful resources are available for someone to sit back and leave the problem to work itself out. False hopes have killed too many people.

One of my (Jim's) favorite stories in the Old Testament is the one about Joshua, Caleb, and the other ten spies who explored the promised land of Canaan. They found a land "flowing with milk and honey," just as God had promised the Israelites when they were captive in Egypt. The spies reported the abundance and beauty of this land to Moses, but they also said emphatically, "We will never be able to conquer the powerful people of this great land. It would have been better to die in Egypt."

There was, however, a minority report. Joshua and Caleb said, "We should go up and take possession of the land, for we can certainly do it" (Num. 13:30).

What was the difference between the majority of the spies and Joshua and Caleb? They saw the same problems and opportunities. The majority report said the situation was overwhelming. The minority report stated that with God's help and a plan, they could face the enemy and succeed. History tells us Joshua and Caleb were right.

Dealing with the drugs at your doorstep can be overwhelming. However, like Joshua and Caleb, with God's help and a plan, you can succeed.

CHAPTER THREE

Road Blocks and Building Blocks

Every thirty minutes in the United States:

- 29 kids will attempt suicide.
- 57 adolescents will run away.
- 14 teenagers will give birth out of wedlock.
- 22 teenage women will get abortions.
- 685 teenagers will use some form of narcotic.
- 188 young people will abuse alcohol.[1]

When you multiply these statistics over a year, a week, or even a day, it's easy to see that families are suffering. These kids are our neighbors, friends, relatives, and even members of our own families.

If we want to drug-proof our children, we must become students of the rapidly changing culture. Our children are being raised in a very different culture from that facing any previous generation. One youth minister put it this way: "Yes, we were eight, eleven, thirteen, and fifteen, but we were never their age." Our kids experience so much more so early in their lives. The average age of first drug use is now thirteen; of first alcohol use, twelve. One in three fourth graders polled by the *Weekly Reader* reported feeling pressured by others to drink, and the figures increased steadily as the kids got older:

Pressure to Drink

- grade 5   39%
- grade 6   46%
- grade 7   61%
- grade 8   68%
- grades 9-12   75%[2]

We were never their age!

The Revolution of Change

We don't mean to be alarmists. Some kids are choosing not to be involved in drug and alcohol abuse. However, parents must have the facts to do the best job possible raising their children in a healthy home.

In this chapter we will talk about two questions: why do kids act the way they act, and what can we do to create a positive, drug-free environment?

My (Jim's) daughter Christy is five years old. As a kindergartner she is experiencing a whole new world of beauty, as well as pressures, outside our home. Taking her first steps into the insecurity of the world around her, what will she see? What will she experience? What will the world be like by the time she graduates from high school at the turn of the century? Let's take a look at several potential roadblocks to sobriety in the society in which our young people live.

1. The Substance Abuse Revolution

Christy will grow up in a world offering mixed messages about drugs and alcohol. On the one hand, she will hear that substance abuse is America's number-one problem. Politicians, pastors, teachers, parents, and sports figures are working to stop this menace. Yet the drugs of choice will be more readily available and stronger than ever before.

If she chooses to live out the little jingle they teach in her kindergarten class, "Be smart, don't start," she will be in the minority. Over half of this year's graduating seniors (57%) have tried an illicit drug, and over one-third (36%) have tried an illicit drug other than marijuana. Forty-two percent of our nation's seniors see no risk in having five or more drinks every weekend.[3] Yes, drugs are at Christy's doorstep, and I cannot afford to say it will never happen to her.

2. Media Revolution and Substance Abuse

As 118 million people watched the 1989 Super Bowl game, they witnessed a subtle contradiction. During a break in the play, Orel Hershiser of the Los Angeles Dodgers stood before a camera and begged kids to "say no to drugs." He said, "Losers use and abuse." Yet the very next commercial featured another sports celebrity holding up his favorite beer and saying, "It doesn't get any better than this."

Media have a profound influence on what we think and what we do. America is watching more television than ever before. In 1987-88, the average person watched almost seven hours per day.[4] The most entertaining commercials are the humorous, memorable beer advertisements. In fact, many studies show that the average elementary school child can name more brands of beer than presidents of the United States!

The National Council on Alcoholism says the average child sees alcohol consumed on television 75,000 times before he or she is of legal drinking age. Former Federal Communications Commission head Nicholas Johnson once claimed that TV showed beer being used 24 times more than coffee and 120 times more than milk.[5] Kids receive not only a distorted picture of how much people drink, but they also receive almost uniformly positive images of alcohol: how it allegedly enhances sociability (back-slapping buddies tying one on in a bar) and magnifies sex appeal (starry-eyed lovers gazing at each other over a bottle of white wine).

A 1987 poll conducted by the *Weekly Reader* ascertained that TV and movies had a profound influence in making drugs and alcohol seem appealing to fourth- through sixth-graders. And in a Bureau of Alcohol, Tobacco, and Firearms study, adolescents and young adults heavily exposed to television and print-media alcohol ads were more than twice as likely to perceive drinking as attractive, acceptable, and rewarding as those less exposed.[6]

3. Sexual Revolution and Substance Abuse

Jackie was one of the leaders of my (Jim's) youth group. She was brought up in a wonderful Christian home with parents who modeled their values in a positive way. As Jackie entered the natural experimental phase of her teenage years, she went to a few parties and drank a few beers. She told me she drank because of the peer pressure and, simply, out of curiosity.

One Saturday morning, she showed up at Cathy's and my door. Her eyes were swollen and red; she had obviously been crying for hours. We brought her into our home and calmed her down, and then she told us an all-too-common story.

"I went to a party last night and, really for the first time, drank way too much. The next thing I knew, I was having sexual intercourse with a boy I hardly know. I'm so embarrassed. I'm ashamed. I can't face my family or even God."

How many Jackies are there every weekend? Today's young people are making sexual decisions based on (1) peer pressure, (2) emotional involvement that exceeds their maturity level, (3) a lack of positive, healthy sex education, and (4) a lack of self-control because they are high on drugs or alcohol.

4. Materialism and Substance Abuse

In a recent youth group meeting I (Jim) attended, the kids told each other what they wanted to be or do when they "grew up." One ninth grader said, "I want to be rich."

I said, "Okay, but what do you want to be or do to become rich?"

"You don't understand," he said. "I don't care what I do; I just want to be wealthy. I want a house near the water, a boat, a sports car, and a life free of worry."

I said, "Sort of like the bumper sticker that reads, 'The person with the most toys wins.' "

"You got it," he replied.

My young friend was making the common mistake of thinking that money buys happiness. He was very wrong. Yet it's difficult to convince this generation of young people of that truth.

A young man who was dragged into my office by his parents before he was ready for help said to me, "Can I be honest with you? I'm eighteen years old. I make more money selling drugs than my father does in a job he hates. With all the money I'm making, I can stay high and happy." Today's young people have more disposable income than any previous generation, and they are spending it more and more on drugs and alcohol.

5. Peer Influence Revolution

In the 1960s, the greatest influence on teenagers was their parents, but a major shift has taken place since then. Peers have taken over as the strongest influence. This means we dare not underestimate the importance of whom our children spend time with.[7]

I (Steve) recently wrote a letter to my best friend from high school. His name is Cliff, and I thanked him for being the kind of person he was back then. He never suggested we use drugs of any sort. I count his strong support as a key factor in my never developing a drug problem. But too few kids today have a best friend like Cliff. Too many have friends who want them to "just say yes."

A study of 8,000 high school students in the state of New York found peer drug use extremely important in both introducing children to drugs and reinforcing continued use. Of the students who reported no close friends who used marijuana, less than 2 percent themselves used drugs. Seventeen percent of those who said they had a "few" friends who used drugs were themselves users. Fifty percent of those who reported "some" of their friends were users had used drugs themselves.

The percentage of drug users continued to rise with the number of reported friends who were drug-oriented. Eighty percent of the students who said most of their friends were drug-oriented had used drugs themselves. Finally, of those who reported "all" their friends as drug-oriented, more than 90 percent admitted using drugs. This study also found that the number of weekly visits with drug-oriented friends had an impact on drug use.[8]

Simply put, our children will become like the friends with whom they spend the most time. Young people today live out their lives in "friendship clusters" of two or three best and most influential friends. If Sandy wears a certain style of clothes, so will Jamie and Brooklyn. If Jamie listens to heavy metal music, so will her best friends. If Brooklyn experiments with drugs, the odds are so will Sandy and Jamie.

6. Family Revolution and Substance Abuse

The best predictor of adolescent drinking habits is the attitude and behavior of parents toward alcohol. For example, children of alcoholics have a four-times-greater risk of developing alcoholism than children of nonalcoholics. Generally, children are more prone to abuse drugs if their parents:

- smoke cigarettes
- abuse alcohol or are alcoholics
- take illicit drugs
- use any substance to help master stress
- impart an ambivalent or positive attitude toward illegal drugs.[9]

Because alcoholism is on both sides of my (Jim's) family, I've had to make a conscious decision not to drink. I'm concerned about my potential predisposition toward alcohol, and I'm even more concerned about my children's. If my three girls see Daddy drink one harmless beer or glass of wine, they may think, "Well, Dad drinks, so it's okay for me to drink."

The family medicine cabinet can also have a negative effect on children. If the kids see Mom rush to the medicine cabinet and say, "I feel so lousy I've got to get a Valium," it reinforces the idea that drugs make you feel better. It's much better to say, "I only take medicine when I'm sick." Never say you take medicine to make you "feel better." And if you haven't cleaned out the medicine cabinet for a while, now is the time!

We are concerned, too, about the number of parents who deny their children's potential for drug abuse. Atlanta's Emory University queried 600 high school seniors and their parents about alcohol use. Only 35 percent of the adults believed their sons and daughters had consumed beer, wine, or liquor within the last month. But according to their kids, the actual figure was nearly double that.[10]

In a midwestern school district, while four out of five parents considered marijuana use to be a problem among seventh- through twelfth-graders, only one in five thought his or her child was involved.

In reality, over half the students had tried it, and nearly one-third admitted smoking pot regularly.[11]

7. Self-Esteem Revolution

The primary task of the preteen and teenager is to construct a self-identity. And let's face it: most kids suffer from low self-esteem. They can easily be seduced by chemicals that make them feel good and medicate their pain.

Why do kids have such poor self-esteem? There are many reasons, but we would like to concentrate on a few of the most common.

Physical appearance. Young people are extremely anxious about their appearance. Although most often they want to be their own person and not look like Mom or Dad, they do want to look and dress like their dominant peer group.

One time a young girl quit coming to my (Jim's) youth group meetings. Her mother was sure the reason was drug abuse, and I figured she had some big spiritual problem. Finally, Leslie, her mother, and I got together to talk. With fire in her eyes, glaring at her mother, she opened up and said, "I'll tell you why I don't go to this church anymore. It's because she won't buy me any Jordache jeans, and everybody wears Jordache but me." I almost wanted to laugh, since my imagination had made this into a much bigger event. Yet in Leslie's eyes, it was the most important issue of her life.

When I (Jim) was the only fourth-grade boy in my entire school with hair under my arms, it was absolutely devastating. I cringed every time I had to raise my hand in class or play skins and shirts on the basketball court. My appearance didn't measure up to the cultural norm. Yet by the time I was in eighth grade, I was wearing sleeveless shirts because I was now proud of that growth under my arms!

Losing by Comparison. Another key roadblock to a proper self-image is playing the comparison game. Adolescents invariably assess themselves relative to someone who is better looking, smarter, or more talented. The player never wins.

When I (Steve) worked with psychiatric patients in Fort Worth, Texas, I heard story after story of parents who compared their kids with other children. Many of our patients were living with the belief that they could never meet their parents' expectations or their siblings' standards. They thought themselves inadequate and thus became totally inadequate to cope with life.

Sociologists call it the self-fulfilling prophecy. If you believe you're ugly, you will be. If you believe you can't accomplish the task, you won't. (Fortunately, the opposite is also true.)

Distorted view of God. Many young people have a wrong view of God, and we're convinced this is a major factor in poor self-esteem. For a majority of young people, God is a great killjoy—a God of works and slow to forgive. They see themselves only as guilty, condemned sinners unworthy of love and respect. From the spiritual perspective, their self-concept is entirely negative. The gospel to them is not good news but bad news of condemnation.

Jesus said, "You will know the truth, and the truth will set you free" (John 8:32). We've found that only when young people really comprehend the unconditional love and forgiveness of God are they truly set free to be all God created them to be.

Is There Hope?

Given the realities of our culture and the overwhelmingly negative statistics, the question in every parent's mind today must be, "Can I make a positive difference? Is there hope?" Our answer is an overwhelming yes.

I (Jim) was reminded recently of an old Sunday school lesson about David and Goliath (1 Sam. 17). David was sent to the battle by his father to check on his brothers and report back. When David got to the scene of conflict, he saw Goliath come out to the Israelites and call them to battle. Goliath's challenge was that if any Israelite would fight him and win, the Philistines would serve Israel. However, if Goliath won the battle, the people of Israel would become slaves of the Philistines.

But no Israelite had volunteered. When David observed this, he was incensed that Goliath would mock the living God, and he asked for permission to fight Goliath. He believed that with God's help, Israel would prevail. His perspective was certainly different from that of the others. He could have said, "Goliath is so big I can't win!" Instead, he said, "Goliath is so big I can't miss!"

That is exactly the attitude we must have as we put together a plan to drug-proof our children. Yes, the culture is scary. And, frankly, we have some struggles ahead of us. However, with God's help and a deep desire to make a difference, we can prevail.

To that end, we have put together six building blocks to form a solid foundation for growth. You won't find any gimmicks or the latest parenting fad. These six blocks are what we have seen work over the years not only to keep kids drug free but also to help them make a positive impact on the world.

1. Give your children time and attention.

Perhaps the biggest problem in parenting today is the overcommitment and fatigue of parents. Coach Vince Lombardi, that "great theologian," once said, "Fatigue makes cowards of us all." I (Jim) know I'm at my worst when I'm overcommitted and tired. Cathy and I never imagined before we had children how much time it would take to raise them right.

The average father of a teenager will spend about forty hours a week working, fifty hours sleeping, seven hours dressing and grooming, but only twenty-one minutes a week talking with his son or daughter. Multiplied over a lifetime, you can see the problem. The average father spends twenty-five years sleeping, twelve years working, three years grooming, and only eleven days and sixteen hours talking with his child.[12]

When I (Jim) finished graduate school in Princeton, New Jersey, a friend gave me a card I've kept ever since. It simply reads, "Jim, if the devil can't make you bad, he will make you busy." So many times I've looked at that and considered it a prophecy for my life. I don't want my children to grow up thinking of Dad only as busy.

Whether we like it or not, our schedules reveal our priorities. When we give our children time and attention, it means we're willing to listen to them. Listening is the language of love. Sometimes our kids don't immediately want the right answer as much as they want to know we're willing to take time to listen. They need to feel important.

I hear many busy fathers say they can't give their children a large quantity of time, so they give them quality time instead. But kids need quality *and* quantity. They regard our very presence as one of the most significant signs of caring.

Paul made a statement important to all parents: "We loved you so much that we were delighted to share with you not only the gospel of God but our lives as well, because you had become so dear to us" (1 Thess. 2:8). Paul loved these people so much he gave them the gospel of God and his life as well. When kids know beyond a shadow of a doubt that they have our attention, they will feel secure.

2. *Give your children integrity.*

A great proverb to memorize is "The man of integrity walks securely" (Prov. 10:9a). We would go a step further and say that if parents live lives of integrity, not only will they walk securely but so also will their children. Kids need parents who will be open and vulnerable and provide good models for living.

A mom, dad, and son were in my (Jim's) office because the son had a problem with lying. Dad was being hard on his son for stretching the truth. The conversation took a different turn, however, when the son said, "But wait, Dad. Last night when your boss called, you told me to tell him you weren't here. Isn't that a lie?"

My (Jim's) life was changed early in my ministry when I heard a tape by Dr. James Dobson entitled "You Can Save Your Marriage." He told his own story of an overcommitted travel and ministry schedule and his consequent decision to cut back and stay at home—to practice what he preached, so to speak. I so appreciated this man's integrity that I made a decision to change my workaholic life-style and make family a priority. It has proved to be one of my best decisions.

We like this little conversation Dr. David Elkind records:
Child A: "My daddy is a doctor, and he makes a lot of money, and we have a swimming pool."
Child B: "My daddy is a lawyer, and he flies to Washington and talks to the President."
Child C: "My daddy owns a company, and we have our own plane."
Child D proudly says: "My daddy is here."[13]

Another aspect of integrity is that when you love your spouse with an obvious commitment, your children will feel secure. Cathy and I (Jim) have noticed that when we do such little things as hugging or holding hands when we walk, our girls like it. We tell them Mommy and Daddy have a weekly date night because we love each other very much and want to spend time together.

We realize not every parent has a spouse. However, if you *are* married, we can't emphasize enough the connection between secure children and healthy, loving marriages. Before many parents can put together a drug plan for their children, they may need to put together a "healthy marriage plan" for themselves.

3. Give your children affirmation.

Psychologist Abraham Maslow said, "It takes nine affirming comments to make up for each critical comment we give our children."

When I'm frustrated with my children, I (Jim) find myself trying to produce in them guilt, fear, intimidation, or some other negative motivation. But what really changes children for the long term is affirmation and encouragement. This doesn't mean we don't confront negative behavior or enforce the rules of the home. However, affirmation is a greater motivator for change than guilt or fear.

More than anything else, our children need to hear we believe in them. Jesus nicknamed Simon "Petras," or Peter. The correct translation is "the Rock." Jesus looked at Simon, an uneducated fisherman, and believed he would become the rock, or leader, of the Jerusalem church. Three years later, who was the recognized leader in Jerusalem? The man who had become what Jesus foresaw. Do your children know without a doubt that you believe in them?

We must look for ways to shower our children with praise. Mark Twain spoke for most of us when he said, "I can live two months on one good compliment." I (Jim) told our daughter Rebecca the other day, "You did a great job cleaning up the playroom closet."

Her reply was, "Thank you, Daddy. I love you." She thought for a moment and added, "I even like you."

All normal human beings respond to praise. In fact, we crave affirmation so much we will do almost anything to receive it. One friend put it this way: "Whoever gives your kids praise and attention has the power over them." If you don't praise your children, someone else will, and that someone could be a drug dealer. Many people with lifestyles contrary to your own are willing to praise your kids to get what they want from them.

4. *Give your children opportunities to communicate.*

"How was school?"

"Fine."

"Anything special happen today?"

"No."

"Is everything all right?"

"Yep."

"Jeannie, the phone's for you."

An hour later, because she hadn't seen her friend Linda for at least two hours and "there was so much to talk about," you have to tell Jeannie to get off the phone.

Communicating with kids is difficult work. Sometimes walking on water seems easier. No matter how frustrating, please don't give up. Do whatever it takes to keep the communication lines open. In the Burns household, my children have special dates with Dad. For some reason, when Christy and I are sitting at McDonald's eating fast food to our heart's delight, good communication flows both ways. Our youngest, Heidi, responds when we go to the park.

A friend had been wanting to talk with his teenage son about God. He had tried at various times but struck out. Then one Saturday they spent the day together putting up a basketball hoop in the backyard. After they finished and had played a game of one-on-one, the son casually said, "Dad, I've been thinking about God lately, and I have some questions. Would you mind helping me understand a few issues?" They sat underneath the basketball hoop and had an outstanding conversation. The communication lines were open because they had spent time together.

Date nights, shopping sprees, games, and special trips are ways of enhancing the communication process. Everyone experiences a deep hunger to feel significant and have meaningful conversation. Parents who keep the communication lines open help prevent deep heartache later in life.

5. Give your children a network.

We are the first generation of Americans to try to raise our children without a network of grandmas, grandpas, aunts, uncles, cousins, nephews, and even neighbors. Young people need a network of significant adults who will listen to them, take them seriously, and make them feel they're part of a caring community. In 1940, approximately 65 percent of all households in America had at least one grandparent as a full-time, active member. Today, less than 2 percent of American homes have a grandparent living with them.[14]

Both of us are actively involved in the life of a church (we attend the same one), and we believe the church family can help meet our kids' need for a network of support. In this mobile age, the church can be a rock of encouragement. We can't think of a better peer influence than a youth group where kids are developing the spiritual, mental, physical, and social areas of their lives in a positive environment.

Do your kids feel they have a network of significant others who can help them through their sometimes rocky path of development? If they don't have as solid a network as you would like, we strongly suggest this become a high priority.

6. *Give your children a spiritual foundation.*

This may sound corny to some, but the old adage is true: "The family that prays together stays together." Although studies show little difference in drug and alcohol use between Christian and non-Christian young people, one of the strongest factors in deciding not to abuse drugs in all the studies we came across was an active spiritual life. The more involved kids were with their faith, the better the chances they would refrain from drug abuse.

Tim and Donna were cousins and members of our youth group. Their families came from the same socioeconomic group, and both families were active in the church and community. Tim and Donna attended about the same number of youth group events. However, by the time Tim graduated from high school, he had left the church and was heavily involved in drugs. Donna, on the other hand, remained active in the church and drug-free.

What made the difference? Tim was a spectator; his friendships and extracurricular activities all took place outside the church. Donna's social life was centered in the church. She dated boys in the group, participated in missions trips, and even volunteered to stuff envelopes.

We cannot overemphasize that kids become like the people who most influence them. That's why we believe active involvement in the church is such an important part of a drug-proof plan.

What can parents do to build a solid spiritual foundation in their children? Nothing is more significant than modeling the desired behavior in your own life. If your children see you possessing an active spiritual life, the odds are high that they will follow. If you come off as "too holy" or never admit your weaknesses, their spiritual growth will be impaired.

A strong spiritual foundation needs to be built on these principles: (1) God loves you unconditionally; (2) you are created in God's image; (3) you are a child of God; and (4) in Jesus Christ, your sins are forgiven. Let's look at each of these in a little more detail.

God loves you unconditionally. We must help young people understand that God loves them not for what they do but for who they are. Because our society is so conditional, most young people—even with a church background—still do not believe God's love is unconditional and sacrificial. The message of Paul to the Romans is still the word for today: "But God demonstrates his own love for us in this: While we were still sinners, Christ died for us" (Rom. 5:8).

God created you in His image. Kids need to know they are very much a creation of God. In fact, Ephesians 2:10 says, "For we are God's workmanship, created in Christ Jesus to do good works, which God prepared in advance for us to do." The word "workmanship" can be translated from the original Greek to mean "poetry." So every person is a special work of God's poetry.

Kids who can say no to drugs, sexual promiscuity, and other temptations are kids who understand that they are God's poetry: unique, gifted, and different from every other person because God created each of us from a different mold.

You are a child of God. Through Jesus Christ, we can approach the God of the universe and call Him Father. We need to help our children understand they are children of God, with all the rights and privileges of any other child of God. In the next chapter we will discuss in depth why kids take drugs, but one of the major reasons is that they need but often lack a sense of belonging. We can help them greatly by teaching that God takes care of His children and wants only the best for them. Here is an excellent biblical principle young people need to hear often:

Ask, and you will be given what you ask for. Seek, and you will find. Knock, and the door will be opened. For everyone who asks, receives. Anyone who seeks, finds. If only you will knock, the door will open. If a child asks his father for a loaf of bread, will he be given a stone instead? If he asks for fish, will he be given a poisonous snake? Of course not! And if you hardhearted, sinful men know how to give good gifts to your children, won't your Father in heaven even more certainly give good gifts to those who ask him for them? (Matt. 7:7-11, TLB)

You are forgiven. Forgiveness is available for the asking. We like to tell kids, "God is absentminded when it comes to confessed sin." What we mean is that He forgives and forgets. "If we confess our sins, he is faithful and just and will forgive us our sins and purify us from all unrighteousness" (1 John 1:9). We are a new creation in Christ (see Gal. 2:20). No longer do we need to be accepted by a crowd, because God has not only accepted us as His children but also forgiven us our sins. And His forgiveness is forever.

I (Jim) wish you could meet Linda. Today she's a radiant mother of three beautiful children. She has a good marriage, an active spiritual life, and more enthusiasm for life than just about anyone I know. But life wasn't always so wonderful for her.

Linda was an illegitimate child and was raised in an abusive home. By the time she was in ninth grade, she had lost her virginity, and drugs and alcohol were regular habits. When I met her as a high school student, she would say, "Life is going nowhere for me, and I've made some very wrong decisions."

Over a period of time, we became good friends. We talked about her background and how her abuse as a child was not her fault. We spoke of hope and change. One evening she said, "But what about all the sin that was my own decision? I can't blame everything on my past."

I explained the essence of the gospel of Jesus Christ and told her, "The old Linda can be buried, and in Christ's love and forgiveness you can be a brand new person."

Her smile was hesitant, but she said, "Okay, I'm willing to try."

We prayed together, thanking God for His forgiveness. When we finished, she looked the same on the outside, but on the inside she was different. And by God's grace she hasn't looked back. She now lives free from the guilt and shame that once permeated her life.

Every recovering alcoholic and drug addict we have worked with has had to come to three important realizations. Only when that person accepts these does he or she begin recovery. When a person accepts these principles early, addiction can be avoided altogether. The first realization is that he or she cannot manage life alone. The second is that God can. The third is that he or she must *allow* God to manage life.

The addict must become involved in the spiritual pilgrimage that all of life should be. Of the six building blocks, the spiritual foundation is the most important. When a spiritual foundation is missing, drugs and alcohol will be used to fill the void. But the spiritual foundation of the drug-proof child prevents the void from ever developing. Help your child build a foundation that will last a lifetime.

CHAPTER FOUR

Why Kids Take Drugs and Alcohol

Snow skiing is one of my (Jim's) favorite sports. Although I'm not exactly ready for the Olympics, I love the challenge of a steep slope filled with intimidating moguls. (My wife thinks I'm crazy.) I'll never forget the first time I skied virgin powder. A stormy Colorado night gifted me with new snow. The conditions the next morning were perfect, and I was the first person off the chair lift. I plunged down on the two-foot-thick feathery winter blanket left by Mother Nature.

To this day I have never experienced more surges of adrenalin than I did when I started down that mountain. I was euphoric, and by the time I reached the bottom, I was on an incredible natural high. Breathless and eager to conquer the mountain again, I hoped those feelings of ecstasy would last forever. I've tried to duplicate the experience time and again, spending thousands of dollars on additional ski trips and just the right equipment.

In many ways, especially at the beginning, taking drugs is similar to skiing fresh powder for the first time. It's an enchanting, intoxicating exhilaration. The experience really does help you lose sight of your problems. Everybody talks about it. Curiosity, fear, and anticipation seem to blur together, fogging the real consequences. Others have tried drugs and say it's great. It looks fun, so why not give it a try?

Kids involved in drugs are like skiers who return to the top of the mountain after a great ride down the slope. They've tried a new substance. They've enjoyed the experience, so they head right back to repeat it again and again. Sometimes they go too far. They drink or smoke too much and get sick, but they try again because it was still the best "feeling" they've ever had. "It's better than sex," they say. "It's better than church. It's better than movies." Once they're hooked, they'll compromise their life-styles, steal, lie, beg, drop out of school, and turn from their faith to get back to the mountaintop.

My (Steve's) skiing experience was not like Jim's. I once boarded a gondola with three other teenagers. When the door shut and we headed up the hill, they reached into their jackets and pulled out three paper bags and a can of aerosol spray. They sprayed the vapors into the bags and inhaled deeply. Asking if they knew how stupid they were did no good. They wanted a high that surpassed the natural thrills offered by the slopes.

Experimentation with drugs and alcohol is common. The vast majority of young people will try something, sometime. But besides physical addiction, what hooks them? Unfortunately, illicit drugs have two basic qualities that are terribly appealing.

First, drugs make them feel good. Young people are moving from childhood to adulthood. Their bodies, minds, friendships, and spiritual lives are changing so rapidly that they're often bored, confused, lonely, alienated, or just plain unhappy. For those who don't cope well with all the new pressures, the substance dulls their pain. Sure, it's a false sense of relief, but nevertheless, they feel better and life can go on.

Our children have been brought up in the most drug-oriented society in history. Anything from menstrual cramps to tired blood, baldness, loneliness, and even ugliness can supposedly be cured by a magical pill. "No reason to struggle." "No reason to hurt." "Take this." "Drink this. It will make you feel better." And the little magic substance does make kids feel better—for a while.

One time as I (Steve) sat in a room full of adolescent addicts, I asked, "Why?" After we cut through the garbage, there was 100 percent agreement: pain. Kids are living in emotional pain, and they want relief. But these kids, instead of finding real relief, became addicted.

The second reason drugs are so appealing to kids is that they believe they work every time. To them, drugs and alcohol are dependable, while family and friends, unfortunately, often are not. If kids are worried about family struggles, grades, loss of a sweetheart, or whatever, they count on the drugs or alcohol to make the hurt go away temporarily.

Six Key Factors Leading to Drug and Alcohol Abuse

To prevent our children from becoming statistics, we must have a clear understanding of how kids get started misusing drugs and alcohol. Experts estimate that between 85 and 95 percent of teenagers will experiment with them. It's unrealistic to think they can be sheltered. Sometimes we see parents who seem to do everything right, but their kids are still substance abusers. More often, mental health professionals agree, the route to heavy substance abuse is mapped by the complex interplay of several factors. Here are six major, additional reasons kids abuse drugs and alcohol.[1]

1. Biological predisposition. It's almost universally agreed that a genetic predisposition to chemical dependency exists. Certain kids get hooked much faster than is normal. These kids *must* be told that because of their family background, they simply don't have the freedom to experiment. If you go into any drug and alcohol treatment center, usually 50 percent of the patients come from families where a parent is an alcoholic. If both parents are alcoholics, the risk is even higher.

We both have opportunities to speak to thousands of young people each year, and we've found that when kids are presented with the biological risk factor, they are more willing to change than when presented with scare tactics. When teenagers watch movies about substance abuse complete with gory accidents and horrible stories, they often dismiss them with, "That will never happen to me." However, when confronted with the fact that many experts believe some people are genetically prone to alcoholism, the kids take notice. They want to talk. They want to find out more. They want to tell their stories.

2. Peer pressure. Perhaps the strongest motivator for a young person is the desire for acceptance by peers. As mentioned in chapter 3, if your children's friends are experimenting with drugs or alcohol, the odds are great that your kids are also. If you suspect your children have a drug problem because of the actions of their friends, don't wait for it to get better. It usually won't. Remember, where there's smoke, there's fire.

One of my (Jim's) graphic memories is of the first party I attended in junior high. I had been invited to the party at the home of the most popular girl in our school. My dream of acceptance into that group had become a reality. I was honored, I was nervous, and this was the crowd I badly wanted to be accepted into forever.

As the party progressed, I noticed some of the kids kept going out to the front yard and then rushing to the back patio looking as if they had a special secret. Out of curiosity, I followed them the next time they went. I found Andrew with a bottle of tequila, pouring drinks for everyone, and this time he included me. I didn't want to drink, but the desire to be accepted was definitely more powerful than the desire not to drink. So I did what a majority of kids do. I drank the whole cup in one gulp. It ruined my time at the party. I hated the taste. I went home and threw up!

We can't simply assume our children will say no because we told them to do so. We must help them understand the influence their friends have on them. We must help build their self-esteem, because kids with a positive self-image stand up better against peer pressure. And we must take the time to get acquainted with our children's friends.

After twelve years of moving every few years, we (Jim and Cathy) decided it was time to settle down and stay awhile. We looked for a neighborhood with lots of kids our children's age and chose a house conducive to children coming over and playing in the yard. We picked the house because we wanted to have our home "open to our children's world." Frankly, we wanted to know our kids' friends. Instead of spending money on appearance (after four years we still didn't have curtains in the living room), we invested in swing sets. Sometimes we get tired of being "Grand Central Station," but we're confident we know our daughters' friends.

The other day our wonderful fifth-grade neighbor, Sarah, came over and asked if our daughter Christy could play. I told her Christy and the girls were at the store with their mother and that I was the only one home. She replied, "Well then, can you come out and play?" I put my work down and had a rousing game of soccer on our front lawn!

3. *Parental attitudes.* The most important influence on a child's attitudes concerning alcohol and drugs is still the child's parents. Simply put, "Children see, children do." In many families, alcohol is a staple. Children never see their parents having a good time without

it. Many kids observe their parents drinking and driving regularly and get a double message: "You can't drink, but it's okay for me."

Despite dangerous consequences, it's common for parents to provide liquor for teenage parties. We've had parents tell us, "It's much better to allow our kids to drink at home and provide just beer for their parties. We always chaperon them."

All studies show that the earlier children experiment with drinking and drugs, the more likely they are to become abusers, because they learn to use chemicals to cope with natural development. If they feel anxiety, they use a drug to sedate that anxiety. Such kids stop learning how to handle stress. So one of the most important pieces of advice we can give parents is "Don't model alcohol or drug use. Period."

Ten years ago, when I (Steve) cautioned teenagers about the problems associated with drinking, they would commonly refer to their parents who drank. Today they refer to parents who used drugs in the 1960s and '70s. These parents often don't care as much about their kids' use of drugs, and some continue to model the role of a user.

4. Life crisis. Like adults, children have to deal with stresses such as illness, divorce, or moving to a new community. As with adults, alcohol and drugs can serve to deaden the pain. I (Jim) recently had a woman tell me, "It wasn't until years later that I learned my son started drinking at fourteen and a half when his father and I got a divorce." This woman was so absorbed with her own emotional and financial needs that it took a tragic accident to get her to see her son's problems.

5. Depression. Professionals who work with children and teenagers are observing a major increase in depression among their parents. The underlying causes of depression are complex, and we won't attempt to give a full psychological explanation. However, we do need to mention that an angry or depressed child is prone to drug abuse.

Some depression is normal among teenagers. After all, the teen years are a time of rapid transition. But certain warning signals can alert us to a problem, and if any of these persist, we recommend you seek professional help for your child. The following signs are taken from the work of Dr. Ross Campbell.[2]

If your child is only mildly depressed, you will notice an inability to keep his or her mind focused on a subject as long as usual. The attention span is shorter; the mind will drift, and your child will become easily distracted. A short attention span may be the first sign of depression.

Boredom is normal for teens, especially in early adolescence, but only for short periods. When children are bored over a long period of time, they will tend to look for stimulation. Research indicates that children of low imagination and creativity are more readily bored, and these children are more likely to turn to drugs. This is why it's important to encourage a child, from a young age, to participate in athletics, drama, dance, music, art, or any other kind of creative activity. If you can keep your child from a crisis of boredom, you can help prevent problems in the future.

Somatic depression is a physiological depression that occurs as young people suffer headaches, stomachaches, or lower chest pains. With the additional stress young people are experiencing today, somatic depression is common, and many turn to drugs or alcohol to medicate their pain.

Withdrawal from friends is another warning signal. Dr. Campbell explains it this way: "She will not just simply stay away from them [friends]. She will become belligerent. . .toward them so that the ensuing unpleasantness will result in total alienation. . . .Your teen will become very lonely and could very well start associating with unwholesome peers. This is where. . .peer influence comes in and can be the cause of initial drug experimentation. But as you can see, . . . depression would also be the cause."[3]

Dr. John Baucom has prepared another list of symptoms of depression to help you determine whether your child is depressed and, if so, how severe the depression is. If you see your child clearly in this list and the symptoms persist for an extended time, seek professional help.

Early Stages

Inability to concentrate

Excessive daydreaming

Withdrawal from friends

Impulsive acts, seemingly without forethought

Declining grades

Change in eating or sleeping habits

Middle Stages

Acts of aggression

Rapid mood swings

Loss of interest in work, school, etc.

Loss of friends

Boredom

Preoccupation with physical complaints

Mild rebelliousness

Sudden changes in personality

Danger Stage

Visible depression

Anorexia

Alcohol or drug abuse

Suicide threats, attempts, or gestures

Giving away prized possessions

Preoccupation with death

Expressions of helplessness

Loss of values

Extreme aggressive behavior

Overt rebelliousness[4]

In an adolescent unit in Orange, California, during a discussion of depression with the kids there, a common thread was the shattering reality that life isn't easy. The kids "hit the wall" when they discovered life doesn't magically work out the way they wanted it to. Many of these kids were affluent; everything they needed had been given to them. It was too devastating for them to face their problems, let alone attack them. In the face of discomfort, they folded up into the emotional cocoon of depression. For many, drugs seemed the only way out.

6. *Parenting style.* Too many parents are intent on being "buddies" with their children and do not take the responsibility of parenting seriously enough. Mental health professionals are unanimous: children aren't getting enough supervision. Far too many parents have given up on investing the quality and quantity of time it takes to create a loving, firm, caring environment.

A mother called me (Jim) to talk about her daughter's behavior: she was sneaking out of the house and getting drunk. The previous weekend the parents had changed their minds about staying overnight at a convention and had come home. "A full-blown, drunken orgy" were the words this concerned mother used to describe the party they walked in on.

I welcomed the family to visit with me as long as I could see the mom, dad, and daughter together at the first appointment. I noticed the three of them arrived in three different, expensive cars. As they began to talk, the parents mentioned they had an expensive house overlooking the Pacific Ocean. They also said both parents worked. Dad left the home at 6:15 A.M. and returned after 8 P.M. They were experiencing intense financial pressure.

As the story unfolded, it became clear that both parents were working hard to pay for their beautiful house, the leases on three expensive cars, and to put away some money for their daughter's college fund.

In the meantime, no one was taking any significant time to parent their needy daughter.

I suggested meekly, "Have you ever considered moving to a smaller house, trading in your expensive cars, and working fewer hours to make your home something besides a place to sleep and fight?" It was as if they needed permission to cut back on their fancy life-style and become a family again.

Months later they called me. They had moved and traded in the nice cars; Mom was working only part-time, Dad came home for dinner, and their daughter had quit her "old life." She was looking forward to going to college after taking a few summer school classes to make up some of the time she had lost to the party scene. I wish all true stories could have such a happy ending.

Dr. H. Stephen Glenn, former director of the National Drug Abuse Center in Washington, D.C., says parents may be overly strict or overly permissive because they honestly feel this is the most loving thing they can do for their children. However, their kids may not perceive the loving part. "Children base their behavior on their perception of what is true, not on what is actually true," Glenn says. "Children are more likely to perceive loving intentions when tone of voice and actions convey dignity and respect along with firmness."[5]

Kids use drugs for numerous reasons. Hopelessness, rebellion, the desire to feel like an adult, are other reasons we often hear. We cannot afford to believe that "it will never happen to our family."

The Path to Drug Abuse

When Terry's parents called to say they wanted to see me (Jim), I tried to talk them out of coming. After all, it sounded like a clear case of drug abuse in Terry's life. They needed a drug treatment program, not me. But they persevered. The day I met the family, I was shocked by their appearance and story.

They drove to my office in their beautiful new Mercedes. Instead of Terry looking like the street person I expected (from the stories his mother had told me), he was a clean-cut young man who was the star pitcher on his Christian high school baseball team. His parents were immaculate, articulate, and extremely concerned about Terry. Both were active in the church, and Terry had been raised in what truly appeared to be a model Christian home. My immediate reaction, even though I knew better, was to dismiss Terry's drug problem as teenage experimental use, wish this family well, and move on to more pressing matters.

It wasn't until I was alone with Terry that I heard his story. At age thirteen he went to a church camp. Some of the boys had sneaked in beer and wine. They were a little older than Terry, but because he was intelligent and a great athlete, they accepted him into the group.

The second night of camp, Terry drank the first beer ever offered to him. He wasn't sure about the taste, but he liked the acceptance of these older guys. Before the week was over, Terry had experimented with beer, wine coolers, and marijuana. He liked the high, and he liked the peer approval. He knew his parents would never approve. As a young Christian himself, he felt guilty, but he justified the experience, saying, "Even Jesus drank wine."

His experimental use turned to more regular use. He found a whole new world of kids who built their social lives around alcohol and marijuana.

Terry also noticed early in his drinking and drugging that he had an extremely high tolerance. While other kids had three beers and either got so drunk they couldn't walk straight, or they fell asleep or got sick, Terry could drink a six-pack and still be "in control."

Terry so enjoyed getting high that he began to think about it daily: "I was always figuring out when would be the next time I could drink or smoke marijuana." Some of his older friends introduced him to cocaine, saying it was the ultimate high. He tried it, loved it, and was hooked immediately. In his own words, "I became a slave to it."

At the same time, Terry was still trying to maintain his "Christian appearance." He was lying to his parents and found himself stealing alcohol from a neighborhood liquor store. Even though he looked clean-cut and could still maintain the appearance of being straight most of the time, his grades, friendships, home life, and relationships with girls were beginning to slip.

Terry was one of the 3 million-plus teenagers who are chemically dependent. He had to get high to make it through the day, and he had a dangerous preoccupation with doing just that. His life had followed the typical stages of change listed below.

FREQUENTLY-SEEN STAGES
IN ADOLESCENT CHEMICAL USE

1. Experimental use
Late grade school or early junior high years

Intake	What the World Sees
1. Occasional beer drinking, pot-smoking or use of inhalants (glue-sniffing, sniffing aerosols, etc.). Usually done weekends or during the summer, mostly with friends. 2. Easy to get high (low tolerance). 3. Thrill of acting grown-up and defying parents is part of the high.	1. Often unplanned, using beer sneaked from home, model glue, etc. 2. Little use of "harder" drugs at this stage.

2. More regular use
Late junior high and early senior high years

4. Tolerance increases with increased use. More parties involving kegs, pot, possibly pills or hash. Acceptance of the idea that "everyone does it" and wanting to be in on it. Disdain of "local pot" or 3.2 beer. Staying out later, even all night.
5. Use of wine or liquor may increase, but beer remains the most popular drink. Willing to suffer hangovers.
6. Lying to parents about the extent of use and use of money for drugs.
7. Use on week nights begins, and skipping school may increase.
8. Black-outs may begin, and talk with friends about "What did I do last night?" occurs.
9. Solitary use begins— even smoking at home (risk-taking increases). Concentration on fooling parents or teachers when high.
10. Preoccupation with use begins. The next high is

3. More money involved, false ID's used. Alcohol or pot bought and shared with friends.
4. Parents become aware of use. May start a long series of "groundings" for late hours.
5. Drug-using friends often not introduced to parents.
6. Lying to parents about the extent of use and use of money for drugs.
7. School activities are dropped, especially sports. Grades will drop. Truancy increases.
8. Non drug-using friends are dropped. Weekend-long parties may start.

carefully planned and an-
ticipated. Source of supply
is a matter of worry.
11. Use during the day
starts. Smoking before
school to "make it through
the morning." Use of "dust"
may increase, or experi-
ments with acid, speed, or
barbs may continue.

3. Daily preoccupation

12. Use of harder drugs increases (speed, acid,
barbs, dust).
13. Number of times high
during the week increases.
Amount of money spent for
drugs increases (concealing
savings withdrawals from
parents).
14. "Social use" decreases—
getting loaded rather than
just high. Being high
becomes normal.
15. Buying more and using
more—all activities seem to
include drug use of alcohol.
16. Possible theft to get
money to insure a supply.
There may be a contact
with "bigger" dealers.
17. Solitary use increases.
User will isolate self from

9. Possible dealing or front-
ing for others.
10. Possible court trouble
for minor consumption or
possession. May be arrested
for driving while intoxicated.
Probation may result.
11. May try to cut down or
quit to convince self that
there is no problem with
drugs.
12. Most straight friends are
dropped.
13. Money owed for drugs
may increase. More truancy
and fights with parents
about drug use.

other using friends.
18. Lying about or hiding
the drug supply. Stash may
be concealed from friends.

4. Dependency

19. Getting high during
school or at work. Difficult
to face the day without
drugs. Drugs are used to
escape self.
20. Possible use of injec-
table drugs. Friends are
burnouts (and may take
pride in the label).
21. Can't tell what normal
behavior is any more—
normal means being stoned
nearly constantly.
22. Physical condition
worsens. Loss of weight,
more frequent illnesses,
memory suffers, flashbacks
may increase. Thoughts of
suicide may increase.

14. Guilt feelings increase.
Questioning own use but
unable to control the urge.
15. Low self-image and self-
hate. Casual sexual involvement. Continued denial of
problem.
16. School dropped. Deal-
ing may increase, along
with police involvement.
Parents may "give up."
17. Paranoia increases.
Cost of habit increases with
most of money going for
habit.
18. Loss of control over use.

Thank God, Terry's family has now seen him go successfully through a treatment center. They suffered an incredible amount of emotional stress and pressure on their marriage, not to mention spending tens of thousands of dollars to help Terry.

Kids who abuse drugs usually get started through "gateway drugs," as in Terry's case. Two studies found a constant progression of drug use among high school students. The pattern consistently followed

four well-defined steps:
1. beer or wine
2. hard liquor and/or cigarettes
3. marijuana
4. other illicit drugs

Researchers report that virtually no one moves to step four without first going through steps one, two, and three. A sampling of New York college students supports the other research. In this study, 99 percent of people who used illegal drugs regularly had started with tobacco and then marijuana.[7]

Tobacco. Eighty-five percent of those who experiment with cigarettes will become addicted to nicotine, some after smoking as few as five to ten cigarettes. Of these kids, 81 percent will try marijuana, whereas only 21 percent of nonsmokers will.

Here is one instance where cold, hard facts speak volumes. According to former White House drug chief Dr. Robert L. Dupont, Jr., cigarette-smoking twelve-to-seventeen-year-olds are:

- twice as likely to use alcohol;
- nine times as likely to ingest depressants and stimulants;
- ten times as likely to smoke marijuana; and
- fourteen times as likely to use cocaine, hallucinogens, and heroin.[8]

Smoking kills more than 52,000 Americans each year through chronic lung disease. Another 4,000 American lives are taken through cigarette-caused fires, and upwards of $30 billion per year are spent on health-care problems related to smoking. Just because tobacco is legal to smoke doesn't mean it's an intelligent choice. We like what they're teaching kids in kindergarten: "Be smart, don't start." In fact, we often recommend that if children start smoking, it be considered irresponsible behavior worthy of a parent's immediate attention.

Because cigarette smoking can lead young people into the world of drugs, should parents smoke cigarettes? That depends on how committed they are to bringing up drug-free children.

Alcohol. Alcohol is a dangerous drug, though our society mistakenly tends to view it as separate from other drugs. Some parents are actually relieved to discover their kids are "only" drinking and not smoking pot or swallowing pills. But alcohol is a drug, a depressant, and it causes more deaths among young people than any other drug. Because it's legal and accepted by the general population, many people are unaware that it attacks the nervous system and, over a period of time, can shorten a life.

Nearly one-third of all high school seniors, however, claim that most or all of their friends get drunk at least once a week. Dr. John Baucom states,

> Approximately 15 million Americans are addicted to alcohol, according to the Drug Enforcement Administration and the National Institute of Alcohol Abuse and Alcoholism. The same organizations state that an additional 4.6 million problem drinkers exist in our country. Over 100,000 people die each year from the effects of alcohol. An alcoholic has a life expectancy 10-22 years shorter than a non-drinker. Up to 83 percent of all fire-related deaths are considered to be alcohol related, and 50 percent of all home accidents are caused by problem drinkers. Alcohol is a factor in 70 percent of all drownings and 40 percent of all industrial accidents. Over 15,000 adult suicides and 3,000 teenage suicides are committed each year by alcoholics. And NIDA estimates 4 million problem drinkers are teenagers.[9]

Marijuana. Smoking marijuana usually becomes the springboard to heavier drug use. Sixty-seven percent of marijuana users progress to other drugs, while 98 percent of those teens who do not smoke pot also do not take other drugs. We went to junior and senior high school in the late 1960s. Timothy Leary and other drug heroes were saying marijuana was not harmful. In fact, they said it was less dangerous than alcohol and caused no hangover. Our generation generally believed this to be true, and at the time no substantial studies proved the contrary.

All that has changed, however. For one thing, today's marijuana is up to twenty times stronger than the plants harvested only a decade ago. Furthermore, it has been substantiated that not only does pot have more cancer-causing agents than tobacco, but it also destroys brain cells and harms short-term memory retention.

Continued use of this drug can lead to what is called "amotivational syndrome": lethargy, reduced attention span, varying degrees of personality change, and general lack of interest in anything but getting high. Marijuana also diminishes the body's ability to protect itself from illness by reducing the division of disease-repelling white blood cells. Therefore, a person who smokes marijuana regularly is likely to get sick more often than is normal. Marijuana is not the harmless drug of the psychedelic '60s but a treacherous gateway to heavier drug use.

A Success Story

Tom and Linda Miramar are terrific parents. If you asked them, of course, they could tell as many "war stories" as the next family. However, five years ago they decided to learn all they could about drug and alcohol abuse. They were typical Christian parents with a desire to keep their three children from experiencing the same pain as their older, alcoholic nephew.

When their two boys and one girl were ten, twelve, and fourteen, they came to me (Jim) and asked for every resource on drug and alcohol abuse I could offer. I gave them books, pamphlets, and tapes and pointed out a few excellent (and free) educational seminars at a local treatment center. Then they put together a plan of education and prevention. They spent time discussing what they had learned with their children. The family made a contract that at the first sign of a problem, there would be agreed-upon-by-all consequences. To be a good role model, Tom even gave up his occasional cigar.

Last Christmas I received a note from the family. It read: "Dear Jim: Concerning our Drug-Proof Plan, after five years, so far, so good. It was worth the investment. Thanks. The Miramar Family."

CHAPTER FIVE

Educating the Right Way at the Right Time

A few years ago, Cathy and I (Jim) were shopping at the local K-mart. I'm a sucker for their "blue-light specials," and that day I found myself purchasing a pair of paisley, multicolored suspenders. They were ugly, but they cost me only $8.49 instead of $8.79. Such a deal! I had never worn suspenders, and Cathy had to show me how to put them on.

I proudly displayed my new purchase at our church youth group meeting the next evening. Since suspenders were not in style, the kids were intrigued by their youth pastor, to say the least. The next week, five students came to our group wearing suspenders. The following week, I was joined by nine others who had made the suspender purchase. (Of course they paid the full thirty cents extra!)

To be honest, I never wore suspenders again. The kids kept coming up behind me and snapping me with my own suspenders. But the experience reminded me again of the power of modeling. It's still the most influential educator. My oldest daughter answers the phone exactly like her mother. And when she's angry, it's an almost-humorous imitation of what I look like when I'm angry.

When in doubt, kids imitate what they have seen their parents do. Like it or not, your children are copying your example. That being the case, we have to evaluate what behaviors we're modeling.

One of the most powerful examples of modeling was presented a few years back in a commercial by the National Cancer Society. A father was shown smoking, and then a little boy of about two mimicked everything Dad did. He found his father's cigarette package, pulled out a cigarette, and pretended to light up. The ad finished with the caption, "Like father, like son."

What do you say to your kids about drugs through your example? Is there an underlying message that you don't think they're so bad? Are your children seeing your attitude as one of indifference? What drugs do you take? Reaching for a Valium or misusing sleeping pills are all part of a drug-taking picture that a child forms with you as the central actor. Are you willing to give up such things so your child can be free of drug and alcohol problems?

Troubled kids almost always point out the problems of excess in their parents. They say things like, "My father doesn't drink, but you should see how much he eats. He's no better than I am. I use drugs, and he uses food." "My mother doesn't drink, but every time there's a crisis, she has to take some kind of pill. Why should she get on me if she has to have her own drugs?"

Whether it's excessive food, medication, or burying ourselves in our work, we parents must examine our compulsive behaviors. Our kids use them as part of a denial system that prevents change. But more important, they model these behaviors.

No message comes through louder than your drinking. Kids are confronted with alcohol every day. It's a common topic of conversation at school and a routine behavior for many kids in junior high and high school. So naturally your children are going to be interested in what your drinking behavior is.

They will watch you for cues that drinking is okay. If you've been making mistakes in this area, it's not too late to stop and let your children see what it's like to start over. No lesson is more powerful than the example of an adult changing for the better.

Many years ago Peter Marshall, former chaplain to the United States Senate, gave a sermon that had a profound influence on my (Jim's) life. In it he told a story that helped me make a decision to abstain from all alcohol.

He told of a minister who was asked to make a patriotic address at a dinner attended by many prominent government and business officials. It was a swank affair, and cocktails were flowing freely. Mr. Jones, who sat immediately to the minister's left, was greatly enjoying the alcohol. When Mr. Jones noticed the minister had an untouched glass of champagne in front of him, Mr. Jones stated, "Say, you haven't touched yours. Why not? Guess I'm rude to mention it, but surely you haven't any scruples against champagne?"

The minister replied, "No, you're not rude to ask at all." He went on to say, "I have a steady stream of people coming to my study who need help. Their lives are all messed up, and I guess you'd be surprised to know that most of them, in one way or another, have liquor involved in the mess. To drink this glass of champagne is no sin. However, because of so many who cannot control their alcohol, I choose to be self-disciplined. I would never want anyone to justify his alcohol abuse by saying, 'Well, the minister drinks.' So I've chosen to abstain. It's not a matter of sin, but rather of example."

What Needs to Be Taught

Proverbs 22:6 tells us to train children in the way they should go, and when they are older, they will not turn from it. Is it any wonder we have such a high rate of alcohol and drug abuse when parents and kids spend so little time on this subject?

Children with the best chance of not doing drugs or alcohol come from families that have taken the time to train. And during the preteen and adolescent years, this is especially vital. If you can get children through those years drug free, their lives are almost guaranteed to be free from chemical abuse. Those who neither smoke nor drink as teenagers are virtually immune to later drug abuse. But parents who refuse to take the time to educate their children have a good chance of spending time trying to treat serious problems later.

The education part of a good drug-proof plan involves more than just knowing and teaching the facts about alcohol and drugs. Those are important, but the teaching must have a broader base, including the following three areas.

Responsible versus irresponsible behavior. When I (Steve) first started working with drug addicts and alcoholics, I was amazed at the level of immaturity I saw. Many of these people told stories of how they stopped maturing when they started using drugs. Others told me they never learned to make decisions based on rewards for good decisions and discipline for bad decisions. Many never had a model of responsible behavior, and even more were without someone to guide them toward it. So our job was to do for them what no parent had done before. We taught them the art of making responsible decisions. Don't neglect this important task for your children.

For example, suppose my (Jim's) daughter comes to me and asks, "Daddy, may I go to the beach with the Foster family today?"

I must help her see the whole picture, so I say, "You would have a great time at the beach with the Fosters. They're some of our best friends, and you're welcome to go with them most of the time. However, we're having your sister's birthday party at the same time.

Which do you think is more important?"

My goal is to let her come up with the right decision on her own. However, I may well hear, "But Rebecca has all her friends coming to the party, and she really wouldn't care if I wasn't there."

In that case, I may have to put my foot down and say, "Today you are not allowed to go with the Fosters, because I believe it's more important for our family to celebrate Rebecca's birthday together." Even though I had to impose my will, I still introduced the concept of thinking and choosing logically, not just emotionally.

Social and communication skills. The adolescent social lubricants of the 1980s are alcohol and drugs. Parents must take the time to teach children, through instruction and by example, to socialize and communicate without chemical assistance. Kids need to be exposed to social situations from a young age and shown how to relate to others in a relaxed manner. The edge of awkwardness needs to be rubbed off by caring parents. Then a child will have less need to find social success in a bottle or a pill.

Positive alternatives to drugs and alcohol also need to be implanted in kids' minds. Parents can help a child find and develop some skill or talent so the child feels competent. Sports and the arts are good possibilities. They build self-esteem and fill time that might otherwise be used to do drugs.

The dangers of losing control. One of the first people I (Steve) worked with was a girl who drank and used drugs. She was raped in a vacant house. Pregnancy, AIDS, other sexually transmitted diseases, and automobile accidents are real consequences of losing control. Take time to explain the possible consequences of drug use to your children. If you don't, they will see only the glamour of losing control as portrayed in movies and television.

All these areas of education form the foundation for prevention efforts that come next. Without education, the prevention efforts will fail.

You don't need to be an expert to put together a workable drug-proof plan. However, you must become familiar with the facts. In the remainder of this chapter, you will find the necessary information to make you a credible source in any discussion about alcohol. The illicit drugs of choice are presented in the following chapter.

Alcohol and Alcohol Abuse

Six thousand years ago, people discovered that drinking alcohol made them feel pleasantly different. Not long after, they discovered just how bad alcohol can make a person feel and what effects drunkenness and alcoholism can have. The problem of alcoholism was recorded in the first set of written laws. In about 3,700 B.C., the first brewery was established by the Egyptians.

Today the most commonly used drug in America is alcohol, and it is the drug of choice among teenagers. The effects of this chemical depend to some extent on the expectation of the drinker. The same amount of alcohol gets one person energized to go out and party but puts another to sleep in front of a television. The setting also has a lot to do with the effect. In addition, alcohol has some paradoxical properties that produce different effects at different times.

Chemically, alcohol has a depressing effect on the central nervous system. If enough is consumed, it will depress the functions of the system to the degree that it will no longer signal the lungs to breathe or the heart to beat. But alcohol can also produce stimulating effects. Because it has calories that are readily absorbed and utilized, a person who has not eaten for a few hours takes a drink and obtains energy from it.

Alcohol is a food, a drug, and a poison. It's a food because it has calories. It's a drug because it alters moods. It's a poison because in large quantities it's toxic. Alcohol is also a very irritating chemical. Pour it on a cut and you immediately feel the irritation—pain. Imagine what effect that chemical has on sensitive nerve cells throughout the body!

Tolerance

Many myths surround the use and abuse of alcohol. But the most destructive of all is the belief that being able to drink a large quantity of alcohol is a sign of strength. In reality, a high tolerance for alcohol—being able to "hold your liquor"—is a sign of budding alcoholism. It's the one thing all alcoholics have in common.

One day we and a teen's parents sat in an office listening to his alcohol abuse story. He boasted he could drink a six-pack of beer without being fazed. In fact, he said he would drive others home after consuming fifteen to eighteen beers at a party. He was trying to make the point that he could handle liquor. He didn't realize, until we explained high tolerance, that he perfectly described his need for help to cure his disease of alcoholism.

Most people have an automatic limiting mechanism that prevents them from developing a high tolerance. Drunkenness, illness, or sleep occur when large quantities of alcohol are consumed. The tolerance stays basically the same throughout life, though many would argue that a growing tolerance is developed over time. It's true that tolerance goes up a bit for most people, but for the alcoholic, the rise is either quite dramatic or tolerance is high from the first drink. In the world of drinking, the alcoholic veers off on a path that has only one end, addiction to the chemical.

Problem Drinking and Drunkenness

Alcoholism is not to be confused with drunkenness. Many

alcoholics have such a high tolerance that they're rarely drunk. They drink a great deal but are often able to stop just before loss of control. A family might live with an alcoholic for a lifetime and never see the person drunk. Only in the later stages of life, when a deteriorating and aging body loses its ability to contain vast quantities of alcohol, do many alcoholics drink until they lose control.

Drunkenness can happen to anyone with any level of tolerance, however. Some people are drunk on one drink. If that's the case, the Bible forbids them to drink, because it condemns drunkenness, and rightfully so. Drunkenness is a big killer in our society.

The Bible clearly states, "Do not get drunk on wine, which leads to debauchery. Instead, be filled with the Spirit" (Eph. 5:18). Drunkenness is a counterfeit for being filled with the Spirit. It's a form of escape and a maladaptive coping mechanism. Anyone who gets drunk is a problem drinker and needs help. The sin needs to be confessed and the behavior changed. Unfortunately, when teenagers drink, most drink to get drunk. That's why teenage drinking is always considered problem drinking. It's illegal, and most of the time it's also immoral.

Alcoholism

Having been raised in Texas in a conservative Christian home, I (Steve) heard many sermons on alcoholism. The preacher always referred to the alcoholic as a drunkard. A biblical passage on drunkenness would be used to condemn that person, implying that the person had chosen alcoholism and would spend the remainder of his (they were always considered males) days in a drunken stupor.

Receiving this perspective early in life, my acceptance of the facts about alcoholism and drunkenness did not come easily. But eventually I learned the truth about the biblical perspective. It's been a great help in understanding alcoholics and assisting them in their recovery.

The Bible doesn't address the condition of alcoholism. It only speaks to us about drinking and drunkenness. Many ministers think of a drunk man on skid row, drinking out of a bottle, when they think of an alcoholic. But that's the exception rather than the rule. Only about 5 percent of all alcoholics make it to skid row. The other 95 percent are drinking and functioning in jobs, schools, churches, and in families. Many people have no idea they are alcoholic.

The alcoholic is any person who consumes so much alcohol that he or she becomes addicted to the chemical. That's what alcoholism is: addiction to alcohol. If we understand that point, alcoholism is no longer a mystery. But the addiction is selective. Not everyone can develop it. The reason is tolerance. People cannot drink enough alcohol to become addicted if they don't have a high tolerance for it. Anyone can abuse the chemical by getting drunk, but not everyone has the capacity to become an alcoholic.

These facts are the reason we've done so little to prevent alcoholism. One approach we use is to tell our children not to drink. But since 95 percent are going to try it anyway, we have to tell them why they shouldn't. Some tell teenagers not to drink because it's against the law. But they see adults break the law all the time, so the law is little or no deterrent. Some tell kids not to drink because drunkenness is condemned in Scripture. That can be helpful, but it does little to help the young person who is unknowingly sinking into addiction. There is a way, however, to communicate in a rational manner that kids can understand the reasons to abstain from alcohol.

The Sin Issue

Some of you reading this are no doubt eager to know whether we believe drinking is a sin. This is a difficult area; Christians hold varied views. However, from our study of Scripture, our work with thousands of young people, and our own experiences, we have arrived at the following beliefs. We don't expect everyone to agree, but we hope this list will stimulate the reader to think through his or her stance.

1. Drunkenness is always a sin. Scripture is clear on this, a fact that can't be rationalized away. Those who repeatedly become intoxicated need to confess their sin and obtain whatever help is needed to overcome it. Parents should sit down with their children to explain the sinful nature of drunkenness and why God has so clearly forbidden it.

2. Drinking is definitely a sin for some people. For the general population, no specific Scriptures forbid the consumption of wine in small amounts. Some Scriptures do, however, forbid consumption if it causes another person a spiritual problem. Whenever a spouse is bothered by the other spouse's drinking, for instance, it's the drinker's responsibility to stop so as to prevent the mate from stumbling. But the rightness and wrongness of drinking is an even broader issue.

In our society, with so much damage done by drinking, many who feel it is okay to drink need to reexamine the practice. Alcohol is a dangerous chemical. Even if one doesn't drive drunk, we now know that alcohol damages brain cells and other body tissues. And for us parents, who have to be concerned about the behaviors we're modeling, abstinence is the best choice.

3. Alcoholism is an issue separate from sin. The condition develops from years of (often abusive) drinking, so sin occurs long before the onset of alcoholism. When a person develops it, compassion rather than judgment should be given. Direction instead of condemnation is needed. The alcoholic—addicted, sick, and irrational—will respond better to the love of a helpful person than to the anger of one who doesn't understand. Is alcoholism a sin? The more important question is whether you're prepared to help a fellow sinner.

The Alcoholism Progression

Most people think alcoholics are weak people who cannot cope with life. That's not true. In fourteen years of working with them, I (Steve) have rarely seen a weak alcoholic. In fact, what I usually see is a person of phenomenal strength and stamina. Only a strong person could go to work hung over, in withdrawal, craving a drink, having nerves agitated and irritated, and still function well for years. Only in the latter stages do I find the effects of alcoholism producing weakness within the person. The results of alcoholism are not the cause of alcoholism. This is best understood by tracing the progression of the problem through the common steps.

1. Tolerance. Tolerance for alcohol rises to a level that allows the body's cells to adapt to the chemical. Alcoholics become addicted to the chemical and process it more easily than other substances. This forms the basis for craving the chemical. Eventually alcoholics do not drink to feel better but to feel normal; because the body becomes dependent upon the chemical, they function better with it in the system than without it. The normal person watches performance decrease as more alcohol is consumed. Alcoholics watch their performance improve as more alcohol is consumed, as long as the drinking stays below the level of tolerance.

2. Toxicity. The delicate chemical balance in the brain is disrupted when it is saturated with the toxic chemical that is alcohol. The liver is not able to remove all the toxins from the alcohol consumed, so the toxins collect in the brain and disrupt its natural functions. Thinking, feeling, judging, remembering, and choosing are all distorted because the brain is sick. Sick brains produce sick behavior.

3. Psychological and spiritual problems. The result of living with a sick brain is a life full of personal problems. If you don't believe this, spend one day on the ward of a drug and alcohol treatment center or one evening at an AA meeting. You'll meet people on the road to recovery whose lives are strewn with damaged relationships. They may have become detached from their spouses and children. The ability to concentrate has faltered, and job performance has declined. Morals have also declined as judgment has been destroyed. And we can expect that these people will feel guilty and alienated from God.

4. Physical deterioration. In the last stages of alcoholism, the body deteriorates. The liver breaks down, the stomach develops ulcers, the lungs stop working, and the irritation of the chemical often produces cancer. The body was not meant to be saturated with a toxic chemical, and over time it breaks down because of it.

Alcoholism is not the simple choice most people believe it to be. Drinking is a choice. Drunkenness is a choice. But alcoholism is more complicated, especially because of genetic predisposition, which was discussed earlier. I (Steve) was amazed to see how many alcoholics had alcoholic parents. Such a predisposition might grow out of seeing a parent as a practicing alcoholic, but I believe it goes even deeper.

Suppose a mother drank while pregnant. The baby would also be drinking (second hand) and could even get drunk. If the mother nursed the child while drinking heavily, the baby would continue to consume alcohol and perhaps start the addiction process.

Some people are born with a high tolerance to alcohol. This ability to drink more than a normal amount could come from a father or a grandfather who had a high tolerance; such tolerance levels are a common thread in alcoholic families.

All these factors hint at a condition that goes beyond the choices of drinking and drunkenness. Alcoholism isn't just a repetition of bad decisions or irresponsibility.

The information presented here is what every alcoholic and budding alcoholic comes to understand. It is the body, not the mind, that becomes addicted to the chemical. That being the case, an alcoholic must stop drinking forever. He or she cannot become smart enough, good enough, or spiritual enough to drink safely. Mental, emotional, or spiritual growth does nothing to change an addicted body. And once the addiction process is started, it can never be stopped. (God can always heal the body, of course, but we're talking about the normal flow of events, not the miraculous.)

The Essential Facts

To summarize, the essential facts we need to communicate to our kids about alcohol, alcohol abuse, and alcoholism are the following:

1. Alcohol is an addictive chemical used in many popular beverages, and as with any addictive drug, if you consume enough, you will become physically hooked.

2. Relatively few people become addicted to alcohol (about 20 percent of the people who drink), because most do not have a high tolerance for the chemical. They get sick or drunk or fall asleep before reaching the addictive level.

3. Thus, the key to becoming addicted is tolerance. In our society, tolerance is applauded as a sign of strength. Being able to "drink someone under the table" is a badge of honor. But the ability to hold your liquor is not a positive sign; it's quite negative, an indicator of developing alcoholism. Those who have a high tolerance while young become adults who cannot stop drinking.

4. Those who don't have a high tolerance for alcohol are subject to problem drinking and drunkenness. Drinking to get drunk is an irresponsible behavior specifically condemned in the Bible. It always causes problems and is always a sin. Drunk driving is the leading killer of adolescents. Drunkenness is also a prelude to getting high on other

drugs; it's called a gateway drug. One thrill is replaced with a more dangerous one. The key is not to start looking for the thrill.

5. A person who needs to get drunk repeatedly needs help. He or she is in pain and seeking relief in a bottle. There are many other and better ways to manage emotional pain, ways that make it diminish, not grow. Drinking to kill the pain only increases the pain when the drinking stops. The greatest consequences of drinking to get drunk are death and lack of developing maturity. Consequences may also include pregnancy and other results of poor judgment caused by intoxication.

6. People who have a high tolerance for alcohol need to stop drinking. If it's early in their drinking, they need to make the decision to stop before they become addicted and cannot stop. If they're already past the point of being able to make a decision, they need professional help.

In relaying this information, you aren't just telling children not to get drunk. You're pointing out why. In addition, you address the alcoholism problem in present terms of high tolerance rather than in terms of the future. Kids don't care what might happen in ten years. Help them see why drinking is a problem today. When they understand alcohol is addictive and high tolerance allows the addiction to develop, they may decide to stop drinking.[1]

CHAPTER SIX

The Facts About Illicit Drugs

My (Steve's) wife and I once took a trip to the beautiful town of Carmel, California. It was in the fall, when all the leaves were turning deep shades of red and yellow and gold. On the way home, we took the long route through Carmel Valley (which I now call the valley of the shadow of death).

While we were driving, my wife was astounded by the colors. Some of the plants were totally red in their new fall coats. My wife loves to do crafts, and as Christmas was approaching, she was already thinking of what she could do for decorations. She convinced me to stop, go over a fence, and pick some of the beautiful leaves we saw so she could make Christmas wreaths.

I picked two garbage bags full of those leaves and stuffed them in the trunk. After the job was done, we drove on to a gas station just down the road. I had drunk some coffee that morning, so I needed a place to fill up the car and empty me. Of course, just like anyone else, I washed my hands after I was done in the restroom. Then I returned to the car to finish the trip.

About thirty minutes later, I began to have some strange sensations. My face started to flush, and my head became light. Something was happening that I couldn't understand. And then the discomfort of a lifetime flared up. I couldn't sit still. I itched and itched and itched as I had never itched before. And I was itching in places I had never itched before. I could do nothing to stop the itching. It grew worse and worse the longer we drove.

I'm sure you've guessed the cause of my uncomfortable and embarrassing dilemma. Attempting to pick some beautiful leaves for my wife, I had picked poison ivy and spread the oil of that plant to places I wish I had not. For four solid weeks, I was taught that all is not as it appears on the surface. Some of the most beautiful and appealing things produce the worst consequences.

We must help our children understand that lesson, because television, movies, and advertising show us a side of alcohol and even illicit drugs that is very appealing. What you see is glamour, belonging, being cool, freedom, and great times with great feelings. Advertisers can't sell alcohol by showing bums on skid row drinking out of a bottle. They don't show pictures of kids whose heads were cut off while going through the windshield of a car driven by a drunk or spaced-out driver. Kids must be taught that the appearance of a thing is not always its reality.

Almost every day a new term is developed for a new chemical substance found on the street. Some of these terms stick, and some disappear quickly, but the drugs are always pushed as a ticket to happiness. That's a lie, and in this chapter we'll give you the facts you need to know about illicit drugs.

We haven't tried to include every term or every bit of information being used in schools or on the street. We have included the most heavily used substances and the most common names for them. It

won't make you hip or cool. But it will enable you to converse in-
telligently with your children about the substances being passed
around. It will also enable you to discuss the dangers of each chemical,
along with why that particular drug is so widely used.

Tobacco (nicotine)

WHY KIDS LIKE IT: Tobacco is a status symbol of rebellion, an ex-
ternal attempt at maturity. Kids with friends who smoke do it to feel
accepted. There is little adult interference; most parents who allow
their children to smoke do so because they smoke. They don't realize
that if children smoke, they are also probably using harder drugs as
well, especially marijuana. Nicotine produces a stimulating effect
until a person is addicted. Once the addiction is set, the person
becomes agitated if forced to go for long without nicotine. At that point
the nicotine becomes a relaxing chemical that reduces the agitation
as it eases the withdrawal process.

HOW IT HURTS KIDS: Tobacco releases many carcinogenic
chemicals into the bloodstream, brain, and central nervous system.
Blood pressure is increased, and heart rate is increased up to 40 percent. Prolonged use may lead to lung and other types of cancer; mouth
and jaw cancer have killed many teenagers who use chewing tobacco.
The first step of rebellion against parents is often tobacco. Nicotine
is rarely the only drug a child uses.

WHAT KIDS CALL IT: Cigarettes, chew, puff, cigar, smoke, snuff.

FORMS KIDS USE: Cigarettes, cigars, snuff tins, and chewing
tobacco pouches.

HOW KIDS USE IT: Smoke or chew it.

Cannabis (marijuana, hashish, and THC)

WHY KIDS LIKE IT: The marijuana high is euphoric for most
users. Its general effects are relaxation and calm. Most users claim it

stimulates and enhances the senses.

HOW IT HURTS KIDS: The drug reduces short-term memory and hampers the ability to concentrate. Acute panic, anxiety, and an intense fear of losing control are common. The more than 400 chemicals in the smoke cause cancer, a risk that is increased because the smoke is held in the lungs longer than cigarette smoke. The drug causes a severe strain on the cardiovascular system, raising the heart rate as much as 50 percent. The mood-altering chemical THC affects hormones in men and causes a temporary loss of fertility. Marijuana users experience a higher level of abnormal sperm. One of the biggest problems with marijuana is that it's a gateway drug into other, more damaging chemicals. After prolonged use, a phenomenon called amotivational syndrome can set in. When that happens, the child loses motivation to achieve, and grades plummet, along with performance in other activities. Automobile accidents are quite common, since reaction time while driving can be reduced by 40 percent.

WHAT KIDS CALL IT: Pot, grass, reefer, weed, herb, smoke, joint, dope, J, buds, bag, dime, quarter, hashish, hash, getting high, getting wasted, getting stoned, getting loaded, Mary Jane, sinsemilla, Acapulco Gold, Thai sticks.

FORMS KIDS USE: Loose leaves that look like dried parsley, black gunny bricks, oval-shaped seeds, black-to-clear liquid, and THC pills.

HOW KIDS USE IT: Smoking roll-your-own cigarettes called joints; eaten in cakes, brownies, or cookies; pipes; and taking soft gelatin capsules for concentrated THC.

Inhalants (solvents, glue, gases, nitrous oxide, amyl and butyl nitrite, hydrocarbons, chlorohydrocarbons)
WHY KIDS LIKE IT: Inhalants are cheap and easy to obtain and use. There is some stimulating effect, along with euphoria. At higher

doses, the user loses inhibitions and sometimes total control.

HOW IT HURTS KIDS: Initial effects of inhalants include nausea, sneezing, coughing, nosebleeds, fatigue, lack of coordination, and loss of appetite. Judgment is impaired, and heart and respiratory rates are decreased markedly. There is commonly a loss of self-control that can include violent behavior. Some kids become unconscious after inhaling, and some even die. Suffocation can occur when a high concentration of the chemical replaces oxygen in the body and depresses the central nervous system to the point that breathing stops. It is not uncommon for kids to choke on their own vomit while unconscious. Hepatitis and long-term brain damage are results of heavy use, along with permanent damage to the central nervous system that can produce anxiety attacks and paranoia for a lifetime. Central nervous system damage also decreases mental and physical functioning, and specific harm to bone marrow, kidneys, liver, and blood is possible.

WHAT KIDS CALL IT: Laughing gas, whippets, poppers, snappers, rush, bolt, locker room, bullet, climax, glue, aerosol, vapors, solvents, gunk, buzz bombs.

FORMS KIDS USE: Airplane glue, nail polish remover, lighter and cleaner fluid, gasoline, paint, hair spray, whipped cream cans, and other aerosol dispensers.

HOW KIDS USE IT: Sniffing directly from source, inhaling vapors directly, or using a paper bag to concentrate fumes and gases. They also use a small, metal cylinder attached to a balloon or pipe.

Cocaine and crack

WHY KIDS LIKE IT: It is cheap and readily available. The stimulating, euphoric effect hits quickly and lasts for five to thirty minutes.

HOW IT HURTS KIDS: Cocaine is the most highly addicting drug known to humankind. When its extreme euphoria wears off, it leaves the user depressed and often suicidal. Frequent violent behavior is manifested, and kids can hurt or kill each other in these outbursts. The mucous membrane of the nose can become ulcerated from chronic use. Injecting cocaine with unsterile needles transmits AIDS, hepatitis, and other diseases. The highly volatile gases used to free-base the drug sometimes explode, and the child burns to death or is severely scarred. Death can occur when the drug disrupts the brain's control of the heart and respiration. Cocaine also causes angina, heart palpitations, and arrhythmia.

WHAT KIDS CALL IT: Coke, rock, freebase, flake, blow, snow, crack, C, toot, base, dynamite, girl, snorting, doing a line, lady, baseball, crank.

FORMS KIDS USE: White or yellowish powder or paste, beige or light brown pellets or white crystalline rocks resembling coagulated soap. These are often distributed in small plastic bags or vials.

HOW KIDS USE IT: Inhaled, smoked, or injected with intravenous needles, or dissolved in water and inhaled nasally from an eye dropper.

Other stimulants (amphetamines, methamphetamines, dextro-amphetamines, and Ritalin)
WHY KIDS LIKE IT: These drugs produce a state of excitation and energize the user. There is a feeling of invincibility. This allows the user to stay up or come out of a depression that might be caused by withdrawal from another drug. Some kids use the chemical to study long hours. Others use it as an appetite suppressant in controlling weight. The high from these stimulants can last up to two hours, giving the user a state of false confidence and pseudoproductivity.

HOW IT HURTS KIDS: Heavy use can cause death from stroke or heart failure. Tremors, loss of coordination, headache, blurred vision, anxiety, skin disorders, ulcers, vitamin deficiencies, and malnutrition are results of chronic use. Excessive amounts can also cause an amphetamine psychosis with hallucinations, delusions, and paranoia, as well as permanent brain damage. Kids easily become addicted to the drugs, as tolerance develops quickly. Users feel a sense of constant energy until the body can no longer tolerate the drug and the child has a complete physical collapse. The drugs on the street are often look-alike drugs that contain little or no amphetamine. This can cause a child to believe his or her tolerance is greater than it really is and leads to overdose when the actual substance is purchased. Toxic chemicals passed off as amphetamines can also cause permanent brain damage.

WHAT KIDS CALL IT: Speed, white cross, uppers, dexies, bennies, LA turnabouts, black beauties, pep pills, bumble bees, copilots, hearts, Benzedrine, Dexedrine, footballs, Biphetamine, crank, lid poppers, wake ups, popping uppers, speeding, being wired, flying, crystal meth, crystal, crystal Methedrine, mother's little helpers, Preludin, Didrex, pre-state, Voranil, Tenuate, Tepanil, Pondimin, Sanorex, Plegine, Ionamin.

FORMS KIDS USE: Capsules, pills, tablets, yellowish and white crystals, and waxy rocks that resemble blocks of paraffin.

HOW KIDS USE IT: Take it orally; inhale through the nose; or inject directly into the bloodstream by crushing pills or tablets, dissolving them in liquid, and heating them before drawing them up into a syringe.

Sedative-hypnotics (barbiturates, tranquilizers, methaqualone, depressants)

WHY KIDS LIKE IT: Small amounts produce a relaxed state similar to drunkenness. The user feels a sense of well-being, with few inhibitions.

HOW IT HURTS KIDS: Large doses can cause respiratory depression, coma, and death. Psychological dependency is easily developed, as well as addiction with its severe withdrawal symptoms of panic, anxiety, and even death from convulsions. This withdrawal can sometimes be more severe than heroin withdrawal. Driving under the influence kills kids because the drugs slow reflexes and impair judgment. Death from overdose often occurs when these chemicals are mixed with other drugs, such as alcohol.

WHAT KIDS CALL IT: Downers, barbs, blue devils, red devils, yellow jackets, yellows, Nembutal, Seconal, Amytal, Tuinals, Q's, ludes, rainbows, candy, tooies, doing downers, on downs, Doriden, Quaaludes, Valium, Librium, Equanil, Miltown, Serax, Tranxene, Zanax.

FORMS KIDS USE: Capsules in colors of white, yellow, red, blue, red-and-blue; liquid; powder; tablets; suppositories.

HOW KIDS USE IT: Pills and capsules are taken orally or crushed, dissolved, heated in liquid, and then injected.

PCP (phencyclidine)

WHY KIDS LIKE IT: The drug produces a sense of distance and estrangement and at times an intense hallucinogenic state full of colors and sounds.

HOW IT HURTS KIDS: Since the drug blocks pain receptors, self-inflicted injury is common during violent PCP episodes. Chronic use will cause permanent brain damage, including impaired memory and speech. Paranoia and even homicidal episodes are frequent. Other mood disorders such as anxiety and depression are also common. When large doses are consumed, convulsions, coma, heart and lung failure, and ruptured blood vessels in the brain can kill the user. Psychiatric treatment is often needed when PCP psychosis sets in.

WHAT KIDS CALL IT: PCP, Phencyclidine, angel dust, love boat, lovely, hog, killer weed.

FORMS KIDS USE: Tablets, rock crystal, white powder, and liquid.

HOW KIDS USE IT: Injected, taken orally, or smoked when sprayed on cigarettes, marijuana joints, or parsley.

LSD (lysergic acid diethylamide)
WHY KIDS LIKE IT: Ingestion produces hallucinations and a trip that kids hope will be exhilarating rather than terrifying.
HOW IT HURTS KIDS: Bad trips can result in self-destructive behavior, severe panic, confusion, suspicion, anxiety, and loss of control. Flashbacks can cause a repeat of the destructive consequences. Organic brain damage can also result from heavy use.
WHAT KIDS CALL IT: LSD, acid green, red green, white lightning, blue heaven, sugar cubes, microdot.
FORMS KIDS USE: Blotter paper or stamps impregnated with the chemical, a thin square of gelatin, clear liquid, or brightly colored tablets.
HOW KIDS USE IT: Orally, licked off paper, placed in the eyes (liquid), or eaten in gelatin form.

Mescaline, peyote, psilocybin, and other hallucinogens
WHY KIDS LIKE IT: The chemical is ingested in search of a pleasant, illusionary trip of bright colors and intensified sounds.
HOW IT HURTS KIDS: Bad trips cause panic, confusion, suspicion, anxiety, total loss of control, destructive and suicidal behavior. Long-term use can produce organic brain damage such as memory impairment, confusion, and difficulty with abstract thinking. Psychotic behaviors are common.
WHAT KIDS CALL IT: Mesc, buttons, cactus, magic mushrooms, mushrooms, STP, DMT.
FORMS KIDS USE: Tablets, capsules, and hard brown disks; fresh or dried whole, chopped, or ground brown mushrooms.
HOW KIDS USE IT: Tablets and capsules are taken orally; disks are

chewed, swallowed, or smoked.

Narcotics (heroin and prescription drugs)
WHY KIDS LIKE IT: The initial euphoric high is accompanied by a feeling of relaxation and relief from anxiety.
HOW IT HURTS KIDS: Death can come from overdose, and addiction is almost guaranteed from repeated use. Death can also result from convulsions in an overdose or through the withdrawal process. AIDS, hepatitis, and other diseases are transmitted by dirty needles. The unpredictability of the strength of the drug can also lead to death from overdose since the Mexican brown heroin can be as much as forty times stronger than the more common white powder.
WHAT KIDS CALL IT: Snow, H, smack, stuff, junk, Harry, boy, China white, c-and-w, balloon, dope, horse, white, brown, mud, gum, chiva, being wasted, being stoned, slamming, banging, shooting up, on the nod, nodding, cooking, black tar, dolophine, methadone, amidone, codeine, pectoral syrup, pethidine, Mepergan, paregoric, Parepectolin, Dover's powder, Percocet, Percodan, Fentanyl, Darvon, Talwin, Lomotil.
FORMS KIDS USE: Capsules, tablets, white crystals, liquid, dark brown sticky bars, powder.
HOW KIDS USE IT: Injected, orally, smoked, or eaten.

Designer drugs (Ecstasy, analogs)
WHY KIDS LIKE IT: These drugs produce exhilarating feelings of warmth and confidence. Hallucinogenic effects are sometimes experienced.
HOW IT HURTS KIDS: Since these are analogs, or molecular derivatives, of chemicals such as PCP, amphetamines, Fentanyl, and Meperidine, all the dangers of the original chemicals are inherent in these drugs, but there is an added unpredictability to these. Permanent

brain damage is noted in many users. Overdose is common, because the drug's strength is so unpredictable. Users may also experience symptoms similar to those of Parkinson's disease, such as uncontrollable tremors, drooling, impaired speech, and paralysis. Addiction is frequent.

WHAT KIDS CALL IT: MDA, MDMA, Eve, MMDA, Ecstasy, MDEA, MPTP, MPPP, PEPAP, XTC, TMA, STP, PMA, DOB.

FORMS KIDS USE: White or white-gray powder, capsules, and tablets.

HOW KIDS USE IT: Orally, injected, and inhaled through the nose.

What You See Is Not What You Get

In addition to helping your children realize the hazards of the above drugs, you can help them understand the principle I (Steve) described at the beginning of the chapter: What you see is not always what you get. Something that on the surface looks highly appealing may prove to be a source of great pain.

In the case of crack cocaine, for instance, what many people see is an intense high, which is available and affordable to almost everyone. A pusher turns on a kid, promising the good life, the opportunity to make his or her own decisions and be captain of his or her own ship. The naive child doesn't see crack for what it really is. The pusher is an advertiser for a drug cartel making millions of dollars by getting kids hooked. What the child sees is a beautiful, white powder offering instant pain relief and euphoria. What isn't seen is that the same substance also has the power to kill through overdose, heart failure, and suicide. And the lives it doesn't take it will destroy in other ways, perhaps through loss of jobs or the breaking up of marriages.

Talk to those on death row who have killed in the depths of depression once the crack high wore off. They'll tell you to look beyond the hype and consider the consequences.

If children can learn to think things through for themselves, they will possess a great drug prevention tool—particularly if they figure out the key principle that what you see is not always what you get. Examples of this principle are all around us. I once ordered a wave machine out of a catalogue that guaranteed to make my house sound like the ocean. Instead it sounded like pure radio static, and Sandy made me send it back. Products rarely deliver what the ads promise. Barbie dolls always come with the clothes sold separately. You don't get the full wardrobe shown on television. And G.I. Joe can never do as many tricks as the ads show.

Appearances are not reality in the programs on television, either. What you see on television is rarely what you see in real life. Kids watch "The Cosby Show" and see a perfect family that never has a problem Theo cannot get out of within thirty minutes. But the kids watching may come from dysfunctional families destroyed by alcohol and drugs, where child abuse and neglect are the norm. What you see is not what you get on television, in advertisements, by picking a bunch of leaves, or in taking drugs.

The Essential Facts About Drug Abuse

Educating your children about drug abuse is simple. The essential facts are few:

1. The use of any controlled substance not prescribed by a physician is drug abuse. Using any over-the-counter substance without adhering to the manufacturer's directions is also drug abuse. In 90 percent of the cases with kids, any drug use is drug abuse.

2. The use of prescription medications, even when prescribed by a physician, is drug abuse in the following cases: (a) when false symptoms are presented to manipulate a prescription from the physician;

(b) when the drug is used to relieve discomfort that needs to be pro-cessed over time through various forms of therapy and spiritual deci-sions; (c) when a physician prescribes a drug rather than taking the time to help with an emotional problem or refer a patient to someone who will; (d) almost always, when a prescription sleeping medication is used over a period greater than two months.

Kids also need to understand the following concepts:

1. Adult drug abuse does not justify kids' use of drugs. Parents are wrong to use mood-altering chemicals, and that wrong should be recognized by kids.

2. The glamorous portrayal of drugs in movies does not justify kids' use of drugs. Nothing in life is free. Drug use has a cost higher than the purchase price. That price is called consequences, which the movies rarely show.

3. Behind every use of a chemical is pain. Drug use by other kids who demonstrate little evidence of problems does not justify their use. One doesn't know from a person's outward appearance what pain that individual is experiencing. This agony may come from feeling rejected, from low self-esteem, from a broken home, or from a thou-sand other sources. No matter what its cause, the pain is always there. No one does drugs just for the fun of it. That's what users want to believe, and that's what the media often portray. But it's a lie. People misuse drugs because they hurt, and the drugs are a way of treating that hurt.

There is never a right reason for a child to abuse a chemical. Some people believe early experimentation with drugs is only normal. But those who believe kids should be allowed to explore drugs deceive themselves and their children. Many times they are guilty parents who are reacting to their own past and inflicting their problems on their children. Remember, kids who don't smoke or drink through their high school years are virtually immune to the appeal of drugs later in life. On the other hand, those who experiment with drugs are the ones who go on to abuse them. The place to stop drug abuse is before it starts.

One of the worst things to happen to our country was the acceptance of the lie that there is such a thing as recreational drug use. There is not. There is drug abuse and drug addiction. No third category exists.

If a person uses a drug long enough and often enough, he or she will become addicted. In the case of alcohol, about 20 percent of regular users become addicted. In the case of other drugs, about 90 percent of regular users become addicted. With alcoholism, addiction usually occurs in the minority over a long time. With crack cocaine, addiction occurs in the majority over a short period. That's why alcohol is legal and other substances are not; the risks are much greater with other drugs. This doesn't justify the use of alcohol, however. All the chemicals we've discussed here are addictive. To use any of them is risky. To use a drug like crack cocaine is both risky and stupid.

Follow the Leader

The other day, as I (Steve) watched some children play follow-the-leader, I realized that everyone in the world knows how to play that game. You don't need to be taught the rules. They're inbred. When a leader starts playing, people instinctively start following. Then I realized we never stop playing the game. We follow some leader all our lives. It might be money, career, or a close friend whose approval we desire. So it's important to be careful what leader you choose and important to help your children pick the right one.

As a parent, you serve as a powerful leader to your kids. Be sure you're not leading with old attitudes about a new challenge. The drug and alcohol problems of previous generations are not the same as those of our kids today. Don't make the mistake of thinking that because you lived through it, your children certainly will also.

Two thousand years ago, Jesus Christ came in the flesh and told us to follow Him. In Matthew 4:19, for example, on seeing Peter at the Sea of Galilee, Jesus spoke His first words to Peter: "Follow me." Those were also the last words He spoke to Peter (John 21:19). Jesus wants us, likewise, to follow Him. No child ever followed Christ to do drugs. No child ever followed Christ into drunkenness.

If you have decided to take the time to teach your children about drugs and alcohol, don't forget the most important lesson of all. Teach your children to follow Christ. If they learn to live as He lived, their adolescent years will be free of irresponsibility, drunkenness, and drugs. But we must return to the beginning of the education process. No greater teaching tool—for good or ill—can be found than personal example. If you aren't following Christ, your children will have a difficult time figuring out how to do it. If you're daily trying to follow Christ, however, you're teaching the lesson that forms the best foundation for prevention.

CHAPTER SEVEN

Prevention Tools for Parents

"If I had it to do over, I would have looked for help earlier. We would have put together a plan to possibly prevent the heartaches we've experienced from Tina's drug addiction. We just kept wishing it away, and it kept getting worse" (Tina's mom).

"When I was Reuben's age, I never heard of kids ditching school to take drugs and drink. Maybe I was naive, but I don't think it happened as often. Chemical abuse scares me to death, because I have no idea what to do" (Reuben's father).

"If I had the knowledge and skills to talk with my children, I think I could help them. Frankly, I don't know how to approach them" (mother of three: Joshua, age five; Frank, age eight; Linda, age twelve).

"Janet's problems with drugs and alcohol took us completely by surprise. We assumed her church youth group and school would teach her everything she needed to know to stay away from substance abuse. She was the 'perfect child'—active in church, a good student, and so compliant when it came to obeying us" (Janet's mom).

If you're like us, many times you feel overwhelmed as a parent. You feel that the battle is too difficult, the victories too few. You start to think you can't do anything to help your children make good decisions. Heredity or fate, you tell yourself, has already determined the outcome of your kids' future. You've tried most of the methods you've found in magazines and books, and those techniques sounded great, but they didn't work for your children.

Take heart; don't give up. You can help provide your children with a bright future full of choices. By your actions, you can help them avoid a multitude of problems, including alcoholism and drug addiction. Of course no plan is foolproof. But we believe that the information and ideas presented here can provide your kids with the greatest opportunity to grow up clean. As parents, we can't prevent problems in 100 percent of the cases, but we can radically decrease the likelihood of drug use by our children. As you implement this plan, we believe you'll see hoped-for changes in your children. It will enable them to avoid the destructive behaviors you have prayed they would resist.

You

As we've said before, your example is the most important tool for preventing your children from using drugs and alcohol. Studies show that many factors influence teens' drug-use decisions, but that parental attitudes and actions can influence them most. So ask yourself the following questions:

- Is your medicine cabinet full of mood-altering chemicals?
- Do you medicate yourself with prescription drugs or alcohol any time you feel distress or pain?

- Do you routinely need an after-work drink or an after-dinner smoke?
- Do you hang onto prescription drugs, just in case, rather than throw them out when the problem subsides?
- Do you laugh at drunken behavior on television or in movies?
- Do you wear, or allow to be worn, T-shirts or caps that have drug-related images or alcohol advertisements?
- Does the music in the house glamorize or trivialize drug or alcohol use?
- Do you lack respect for the law and refuse to observe all driving regulations?

If you find yourself answering yes to most of these, you need to make some changes in order to be the most effective prevention tool possible.

The key to being an effective prevention tool is being a "parent in process." That means you don't claim to have all the answers. It means you're willing to admit to your children when you've made mistakes. By word and deed, you convey the idea that in your family, everyone is growing, making mistakes, confessing those errors, learning from the experience, and receiving encouragement to try again.

Sandy and I (Steve) have a five-year-old boy who lives with us. We make sure he hears us apologize to each other. When he makes a mistake, we want him to know it's okay and there's a way out.

Whenever I work late, I call Sandy to tell her when I'll be home. One evening, however, I forgot to call. And when I arrived, it was obvious from her face and the look on Collin's that I was in a bit of trouble. Immediately I realized my mistake and asked her in front of Collin if she would forgive me. Her frown turned a little more toward a smile as she said she would. Then I asked her the question I always ask after making a major blunder: What time did she think the forgiveness would be coming in? As she said "One hour," Collin's grin covered his face. By acting this way in front of him, we were giving him the gift of starting over.

Often children make irrational decisions based on impulse. This is typical of a first drink. Under pressure, they succumb. If they've been brought up in an atmosphere of rigidity, they may feel trapped in the behavior, even though they want to stop, because children who never see their parents admit mistakes tend to feel a person can't turn back from bad decisions. Fear of punishment if the wrong is confessed will also motivate kids to justify the action rather than admit it, be free from the guilt, and move on. So show your children how to make good decisions. And when you make poor ones, be willing to admit them, learn from them, and go forward.

This is an area I (Jim) am working on with my family. Cathy says I sometimes come across as having a "holier than thou" attitude, especially around the kids. So lately, when it's bedtime and we pray with the girls, I've been discussing some of my struggles. I'm amazed how our prayer time has changed as a result. When I'm vulnerable, they're vulnerable. When I'm closed, they're closed. Now, instead of praying only for Aunt Karen's hemorrhoids and all the missionaries in the universe, we also pray for sincere personal needs. I've found that our prayer time has become a miniature family support group meeting, too.

You'll also be a more effective prevention tool if you're an active participant in life. Boredom is a big factor in the decision to use drugs. If parents' lifestyles are boring, children are apt to lead boring lives as well. They need to see that life is full of fun things to do. Resist the urge to come home from work and slowly turn into a couch potato. Instead, show your children how to have fun. Hobbies, music, church involvement, art, sports, and exercise are all ways for parents to model alternatives to drug abuse. Take the initiative to stay active with your kids.

As we mentioned earlier, children regard their parents' very presence in a room with them as a significant sign of caring. Your children need large doses of your time, your interaction, playing, questioning, studying, praying, and just being you. Whether your children let you know or not, they crave your affection, love your attention, and seek your guidance. Even in the most rebellious times, your children are begging for you to reach them. Listen to them, and empathize with their problems. Offer solutions when possible; be a part of those solutions. Be sure they know you will always make time for them.

A teenage girl who sometimes baby-sits for us told me (Jim) recently, "My dad seldom spends any time just with me. But when he does, he always takes me to do 'grown up' things. Sometimes I wish we could just go to a park. He thinks it has to be an extravaganza. I'd rather have more alone times together than the twice-a-year big events. Sometimes I still want to just crawl up on his lap and have him hold me like he used to do."

God

Unfortunately, the secularization of values has left today's kids without standards, but God's standards are still best. Too many young people picture God as the great killjoy in the sky instead of their strongest ally who loves them unconditionally and whose deepest desire is for their best.

Some may call us naive or simplistic, but in our experience, people who pursue a personal relationship with Jesus Christ have a better chance of staying clear of drugs and alcohol than those who don't. It's true, as the statistics quoted earlier show, that little difference exists between churched kids and unchurched kids when it comes to drug and alcohol use. However, other significant studies seem to indicate that those who are not merely members but who practice their faith in tangible ways have less difficulty resisting drugs and alcohol.[1] [2]

The same studies reveal that kids whose parents—especially dads—have a visible, active spiritual life are less prone to drug and alcohol abuse. Thus, strong personal faith on the part of parents and kids is a type of "prevention tool."

In the New Testament, the word for "sin," translated literally from the original Greek, does not mean "to break a rule." Sin means "to miss the mark." Sin occurs when a person doesn't measure up to his or her full potential. Isn't that the biggest danger for most of our kids who drink and use drugs? The chemicals cause the kids to miss the mark, destroying their ability to achieve their goals. People are afraid to moralize the drug problem in our society, but that is exactly what's needed. The moral person is moving toward a higher mark. But most people don't even know what the mark is for their lives, much less that they've missed it.

One reason many kids decide not to use drugs or alcohol is that they believe it would dishonor God. You won't find that information in most books on drug and alcohol prevention. But when abstinent kids were asked why they chose to stay clean, many said it would not be pleasing to God. Others said they believed their bodies to be the temples of God and that to use chemicals would be dishonoring to Him. Clearly, children's belief in God and the value they place on Him are determinants in their drug and alcohol decisions.

That God is left out of prevention material is ironic, because mention of Him saturates the literature on treatment. The first three steps addicted persons must take in treatment are to admit they cannot handle the problem alone, to acknowledge God can handle it, and to allow God to take control of their lives. We don't know of one treatment program in the country that doesn't use those principles. Doesn't it make sense that if God is integral to recovery from addiction, He should also be integral in the prevention of problems?

Unconditional Love

Drug-proof kids are kids who are loved. They know that whether they've been good or bad, destructive or constructive, they are loved unconditionally. Their parents don't always feel thrilled to be their parents. Many times we've become discouraged or irritated, and at times we've seriously considered trading our kids in for different models. But that doesn't alter our love for them, a fact we try to emphasize often in both word and action.

Conditional love comes with strings attached. It implies that if you act a certain way or do certain things, love will be given. There's always a sense that if children mess up too badly, the love will go away. When children feel the uncertainty of conditional love, they're challenged to see how bad they can be and still receive love. It's a way of determining their basic worth. Rather than being motivated to greatness so as not to lose their parents' love, they're motivated toward delinquency, including alcohol and drugs. While bordering on the edge of rejection by parents, they seek acceptance in other places, often with peer groups.

You cannot win with children if they aren't guaranteed your love. Drugs and alcohol produce an instant gratification that some children in a love vacuum come to crave. Fill your kids' need for love and acceptance with great floods of unconditional love.

Behavior and Discipline

Children's behavior should be channeled from an early age. Unconditional love does not imply a lack of discipline—just the opposite.

Love means disciplining kids for their good even when it's painful or inconvenient for the parent. That's because children left to their own whims can be counted on to make poor decisions. But through discipline and encouragement, they can learn the boundaries of responsible behavior and the consequences of irresponsible conduct. They can discover the value of delayed gratification rather than demanding instant pleasure. As they're led into responsible decisions, they learn to insure that the long-term results of their choices are not destructive—to consider more than just the initial effect of a decision. And that helps them say no to drugs and alcohol.

Practically, this means irresponsible behavior must bring undesirable consequences, such as increased restrictions. That teaches the principle of cause and effect. If children's performance in school deteriorates, time spent on the telephone could be cut down or eliminated. A driver's license might be taken away. Curfew might be shortened, and time spent with a friend could be cut down.

Parents and their children should establish the rules of the house together. Discipline is most effective if children know the consequences of irresponsible behavior before they act. It's even better if they suggested those consequences.

A few weeks ago, I (Jim) had a mother and son come into my office. The problems were many, but one was that the son kept staying out past his curfew. His mother had threatened and screamed, but nothing had changed. I asked the sixteen-year-old boy, "Do you think your curfew is unfair?"

"Not really, except on special occasions when I want to stay out an hour longer," he replied.

"How about if your mom compromises and gives you fifteen more minutes on certain weeknights and half an hour more on weekends?" I asked. "She must always know where you are, and if you call, she'll give you a ten-minute grace period."

He smiled and said, "Sounds great to me."

I then asked, "What should the consequences be if you're late for curfew or don't let your mom know where you are?"

He looked at his mom and answered, "That's her department."

"Not necessarily," I said. "You seem like an intelligent person with a desire to please your mom. What would you suggest as a consequence if we can get your mom to agree to the new terms?"

His suggested consequences were even more strict than his mother or I would have proposed, so I helped them modify the restrictions. But we had successfully involved him in establishing them. He knew the consequences; after all, they were his idea. I suggested that if, after six months, he proved he could be trusted, they renegotiate the "contract" and give him more freedom. If he continued in his irresponsible behavior, less freedom would be the result.

The tendency for many parents is to protect their kids from the consequences of behavior. Seeking love and acceptance themselves, or out of some other unresolved need, parents often rescue children when the best course would be to let them feel the pain which grows out of an irresponsible decision. Otherwise children remain immature and problems flourish. A tough kind of love is hard to administer, but it is greatly needed if children are to be taught responsibility.

Too often parents are inconsistent in handling irresponsible behavior. One time they're extremely strict, but on the next offense they take a more liberal approach. Sometimes one parent sabotages the discipline of the other. The first properly restricts behavior after an irresponsible act, while the second goes behind the other's back and allows the child privileges. This inconsistency only encourages irresponsibility and arrests development. Parents must be as unified as possible in their approach to discipline.

I (Steve) worked with a boy whose stepfather continually sabotaged the mother's discipline. The stepfather wanted to win the boy's approval, but the boy didn't like the man any better. Instead, the son manipulated the man to get what he wanted. The inconsistency not only produced an irresponsible child, but it also kept him from getting needed treatment for a terrible addiction.

When parents inform children that any use of alcohol or drugs will produce an immediate restriction, they give their kids a great tool for countering peer pressure. When approached with the opportunity to do drugs, a child can respond, "If my dad finds out I've smoked a joint, he'll take away my driver's license for six months. I just can't risk it for one high." Lines similar to those have been employed many times to withstand the pressure to use.

Just as irresponsible behavior should bring greater restrictions, so responsible behavior should bring greater rewards. Help children see the long-term benefits of responsible decisions by providing some short-term evidence. It's hard for kids to understand (or care) that practicing responsible decision-making while they are young leads to responsible, rewarding decisions when they are older. Provide them with motivation through a consistent plan of rewards and trust.

Just this week, Cathy showed me (Jim) Christy's report card. It was outstanding—definitely better than any I ever brought home. Yet my first reaction was to look at the B I grade and say, "I wonder why she didn't get an A?" After Cathy and I talked about it, however, we decided to take Christy out for an ice cream sundae and celebrate her wonderful report card. I had to resist my urge to pass over all the outstanding grades and concentrate on the few that, while still excellent, were not perfect.

This system of rewards and restrictions prepares a child for the real world. When a person takes a job, there's a predetermined salary, and expectations of performance are communicated. But if the person is responsible and does outstanding work, there's the opportunity for promotion and a raise or bonus. Starting early to help your children understand that system prepares them for later life. But the most important thing it does is provide motivation to achieve beyond the level of mediocrity. It's another reason to make good choices.

Control

One of the hot buttons of adolescence is control. Who's going to be in charge? Will it be the parents or the child? The answer develops out of an ongoing negotiation between parents and kids. Even in the healthiest of families, this tension is a difficult part of adjusting to the growth of the children. Kids always want more control, and most parents want to retain it.

In sick families, parents go to extremes. They try to be either overly controlling or too permissive. Overly controlling parents are afraid to let go of the children, which sets them up for rebellion. And one way the rebellion is carried out is to use forbidden substances. Permissive parents tend to have low self-esteem and need their children as friends for support. They set up a peer relationship rather than a parent-child relationship. This lends itself to drug abuse because there are no boundaries. It also makes for insecure children, as they have to set their own limits and usually are not mature enough to do it.

In a healthy situation where drug prevention is a priority, control should be handed over to children as they prove to be responsible. The underlying principle is that when children learn to protect themselves, parents have less need to protect. Young children need protection because they're so easily victimized. But as kids grow older, they should learn how to prevent being victimized by exercising self-control.

Control is a prevention issue because alcohol and other drugs place children in danger of losing control. Children under the influence of drugs are in grave peril. They must be taught the following dangers of losing control:

- Death due to driving while intoxicated or under the influence of drugs.
- Overdose (since it's always a gamble whether street drugs are in reality what the seller said they were).
- Getting pregnant or making someone pregnant while drunk or high.
- Diseases such as herpes and AIDS that are either terminal or destroy a normal sex life forever.

In Titus 2:2, God tells us to teach older men to be self-controlled. If the older men demonstrate this trait to their sons and daughters, the younger generation, too, will learn the value of being in control. One of my (Steve's) friends gave up drinking years ago because of this scriptural principle. He believed that to honor God, a person must be under the Spirit's control, not under the influence of a chemical.

Any child who comes home drunk or stoned is obviously not in control. When the situation occurs, the parents must step in and resume the protective control the child is not able to maintain. Because the child will resist giving up his or her independence, he or she will try to manipulate the parents into weakening their position. But it's crucial that consistency and tough love prevail.

Contracts

Contracts governing children's behavior can be controversial. We don't advise them for every situation. However, when it comes to drugs, they work well. Contracting for appropriate behavior can also be good preparation for the adult world, where people frequently contract for jobs to be done and behavior levels to be met. When kids are twelve or thirteen, you can begin using a form similar to the one below:

Family Contract

In an effort to work well as a family and hold ourselves up as an example for other families, I agree to the following:

1. I will not use or experiment with drugs.
2. I will not drink or make a decision about drinking until I am of legal age.
3. I will attend school unless I am sick or with the family.

If the contract is broken:

First time   Weekend restriction

Second time   Must stay away from participating friends for two weeks

Third time   Family counseling

_____

Son or Daughter

_____

Father

_____

Mother

This contract is a rough example. You'll want to write out your own that relates to your specific needs. The contract can be reviewed and altered at regular intervals. It provides a point of discussion and objective measure of behavior. Children must look their parents in the eye and say, "I have upheld my end of the contract." As children grow

older, the contract should include the following: never ride with someone who is intoxicated or using drugs; never date someone who uses
alcohol or drugs; call to be picked up rather than ride with someone
under the influence.

Besides insuring that children know their parents' expectations,
contracts can help motivate kids to say no to negative pressure.

Friends

On January 12, 1989, the CBS program "48 Hours" showed two
days in the lives of teenagers attending, and some not attending,
school. These were contrasting portraits of kids who did well in school
and those who were skipping school to hang out at a local pizza place.
The principal of the inner-city school obviously loved the kids and was
involved in their lives. He roamed the halls rather than sit behind a
desk. He even went out on the streets to encourage the truants to
return. During the show he said he had only one piece of advice for
parents: "Know who your child's friends are."

As mentioned earlier, studies reveal that the highest determinant for
drug use is whether children have friends who use drugs. If your kids
hang out with friends who are doing marijuana, your children probably use marijuana. Scripture tells us, "Do not be misled: 'Bad company corrupts good character' " (1 Cor. 15:33). It happens every time.

Know your children's friends. Don't let your kids spend time with
someone you don't know. A minimum requirement should be that your
children's friends must come by the house before your children are
allowed to go out with them. Let your kids know their friends are
always welcome for dinner. Encourage your children to bring friends
over; let your house be one of those places where kids like to come.
Don't be so restrictive or intolerant that your children's friends feel
uncomfortable in your home.

One parent had a big hole at the bottom of his bedroom door. He was proud of that hole, because some neighborhood kid kicked it in while playing football in the hall. "You shouldn't let kids trash your house," he said, "but that hole is there because my house was a place where kids loved to come. I know I wasn't perfect as a father, but so far, my eighteen-year-old son has chosen not to drink or take drugs. I knew who his friends were, and they knew me."

If your children have less than desirable friends, refusing access to them will produce anger and bitterness. But you have a responsibility to restrict access. Deciding when and where your child spends time with those friends is your prerogative as the parent, especially if you have conclusive evidence the friends are drug users or drinkers. But more important than restricting access to such friends is communicating your concerns to your children. Tell them why you're troubled by the decision to have these particular people as friends. A poor choice of friends should provide a teachable moment.

In Alcoholics Anonymous, it's common to hear people say they tried to solve their problems by moving to a new community, and it didn't work. However, it might be a more effective solution for kids. Sometimes a child becomes deeply involved in an unhealthy subculture at a particular school. All the child's friends may be drug users. Then the child is caught using or drunk, and the parents have to decide what to do to save the child. In such a case, the best choice may be to remove the child from that subculture by moving the family. We know of a father who took his sons from Dallas to Nashville for this reason, and it really helped.

Moving is not a cure-all or a quick-fix solution. But it can be a vital part of a plan to save a child. Nothing is more important in drug prevention than helping kids pick their friends. Channel children toward healthy peer relationships and you'll be taking a giant step in prevention.

Coping

Alcohol and drugs are used to cope with pain. Escape into a bottle is a common American custom. "I need a drink" is a common phrase in movies. It's no wonder our kids turn to chemicals to cope with pressure, loneliness, and insecurity. They're simply playing follow the leader. Adults have made escape acceptable in kids' eyes. Broken marriages and out-of-control spending are examples of people using escape as a way to cope. Television models escape behavior as well. And if parents can't cope, children won't be able to, either.

The subtle message from all these escapist practices is that the goal in life is to cope. Struggling to hang in there is seen as successful living. We must help our kids find positive methods of coping, but we must also recognize that life's beauty is found beyond the coping mechanisms. A coping mechanism should produce a better life when the coping is done. Drinking makes you depressed, and the next day you'll drink again. Running, on the other hand, relaxes you and makes you less fat. Drugs medicate your loneliness today and leave you addicted tomorrow. But reading relaxes your mind today and makes you smarter tomorrow. These positive alternatives move children beyond coping and into a better life.

Kids who don't use alcohol or other drugs have found creative and productive alternatives. Their parents created an environment that fostered competency and growth in many areas. Following are some of the areas kids can channel their energies into:

1. Groups. Rather than be expected to form couples, kids should be encouraged to have fun and grow in groups. This is why a great church youth ministry is so important. If there's a strong program, there will be plenty of group activities. Camps, retreats, social gatherings, and

Bible studies are strong drug prevention tools.

2. *Sports.* Active participation in sports has numerous benefits. Children can obtain recognition, develop discipline, and accomplish things on their own. The group becomes the team, with its own pressure to work and win. Sports also help a child stay fit, which in turn helps maintain strong self-esteem. Athletic competencies stay with a child for a lifetime. Parents need to be willing to sacrifice with extra trips and car-pool nightmares so their children are encouraged to compete. I (Jim) am convinced one of the major reasons I didn't abuse drugs was my involvement in athletics.

3. *Arts.* Early signs of talent should be encouraged in your children. Buy a second-hand piano. Purchase a set of oil or acrylic paints. Sing as a family. Offer lessons. We encourage taking a class together whenever possible. This will help build a powerful bond between you and your kids.

4. *Hobbies.* Collecting is fun for many people. Don't wait for your children to pick up stamp or coin collecting. Get them started, and see if the hobby catches on. Spare time is best spent with some productive activity kids can be proud of and call their own. Encourage any areas of interest that your children show.

5. *Community involvement.* Today's children are self-absorbed. They see things only in terms of what they can do for themselves or how they can make themselves feel. As an antidote, involve your children with some projects that assist others. Encourage them to help fellow students with their studies. Take them to nursing homes and hospitals to visit. Get them out of themselves and into the lives of others.

Pressure

Pressure is a key reason kids become involved with alcohol and other drugs. The word "no" is a powerful device for resisting pressure and avoiding a lifetime of misery. Teach your children to say it. Show them how to display strength in the face of pressure. Encourage them to flee the temptations of youth. Use some creative examples of ways to say no. For example, when asked if they want a drink, kids can reply:

"I'd have a drink, but I get sick, and I wouldn't want to throw up in your car."

"That's not my brand."

"That's not my year."

"In my family, we just don't drink. It's a tradition."

"I think I'm allergic to it."

"My parents will take away my license."

The ability to say no is the ultimate weapon against peer pressure. Teaching kids to say no is helpful, but showing how, through example, is the best way for them to learn to use it effectively. Children need to see their parents say no to:

- food while on a diet.
- a drink when everyone else is drinking.
- a car that is too expensive.
- clothes that would throw off the budget.
- a movie below the standards of acceptability.
- an activity that interferes with a previous commitment.

You won't be able to help your children stand up under pressure until you can withstand pressure. You won't teach them to say no until you can say it yourself. (See Appendix for "Just Say No" Game.)

You have the opportunity and responsibility to shape your children's choices and behaviors. Your commitment to them can be your most valuable prevention tool against alcohol and other drugs. It teaches your kids to live up to that commitment through the tough times. Modeling behavior that goes beyond mediocrity isn't easy. It requires looking inward to find the areas that need improvement and the will to improve those areas. In the midst of trying new techniques for prevention, never forget that *you* are your most effective prevention tool.

CHAPTER EIGHT

Identifying Chemical Abuse in Your Kids

A family was concerned about their sixteen-year-old daughter. Her behavior was unpredictable, and her attitude was terrible. The parents had smelled alcohol on her breath several times recently. They brought her to me (Steve) to help prevent an alcohol problem from developing. But after a couple of hours of getting to know each other, it became apparent that we were too late for prevention. This young girl had been a practicing alcoholic since the age of twelve, and her parents had never suspected it.

My task was to help them face the problem they had refused to see even though there had been many indicators besides those two times of alcohol on the breath. It was hard for them, as it is for any parent, to admit chemical addiction in their own child. Their lack of knowledge about their daughter is common.

There's a large discrepancy between the number of kids who use drugs and the number of parents who think their kids use them. The belief that it could never happen to them prevents parents from seeing or acknowledging their children's involvement (see chart, below). But parents who deny the reality keep their kids from getting needed help. That's why it's best to look for the problem rather than expect that your children will escape it. If you're not looking for it, you often won't find it. And if you don't know what to look for, you certainly won't identify early use.

PARENTS UNDERESTIMATE DRUG USAGE[1]

Parents underestimate their kids' drug and alcohol use, according to an Emory University School of Medicine survey. The researchers asked 402 seniors if they had used various substances in the last 30 days. Parents were asked if they thought the seniors had used the same substances in the last 30 days. Parents estimated alcohol and drug usage consistently lower than actual senior usage.

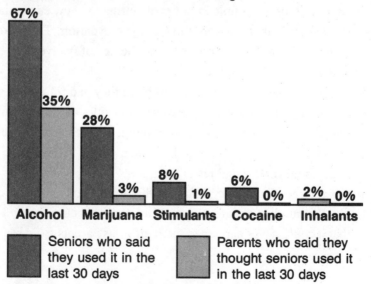

Seniors who said they used it in the last 30 days		Parents who said they thought seniors used it in the last 30 days

This chapter is designed to help you identify the problem as early as possible. The sooner drug or alcohol use is detected and action is taken, the better the chances for changing behavior.

First, let's lay out some generalities about kids who stay sober. If your children aren't using drugs, the following will usually be true:

1. You're able to communicate with them. Few barriers prevent either of you from expressing your feelings or ideas. Your children want to hear your opinions.

2. You know and approve of your children's friends. They aren't mysterious characters who never come around. They even participate in some of your family events, such as meals or trips. You're their friend, too.

3. Your children perform adequately and consistently in school. They may not be geniuses, but there are few failures and many successes. Attendance is not a problem, and their teachers like having them in class.

4. Your kids are involved with healthy activities outside of school. Their interests are varied, and new things are accepted as challenges. They're not stuck in a rut always doing the same things with the same people. They probably enjoy church groups.

5. Your children smile, laugh, and are involved with the family. They have their private spaces, but there's little suspicious behavior. Sulking alone is rare.

6. The way your kids dress may not be what you would choose, but they are fairly clean and neat. Their clothing certainly is not the most radical dress of anyone in school, and it's free of drug paraphernalia and images.

7. Your children have the ability to say no. You can recall several times when you heard them turn down invitations, and they don't usually let friends talk them into things they

really don't want to do. They have relatively strong self-esteem.

8. Your kids are honest with you. You rarely catch them in a lie, and if you do, it's about a minor matter. What you hear about your children from others is consistent with what you know of them.

9. Your children's moods are relatively stable. You rarely see large swings from intense anxiety to deep depression.

10. Your kids openly communicate a consistent message that they don't do drugs, their friends don't do drugs, and they disapprove of doing drugs. When they discuss others who abuse drugs, it's with sadness.

Your children, even if drug- and alcohol-free, won't exhibit all ten traits. No child is perfect, and no cookie cutter fits every adolescent. But an abstinent young person will exhibit most of these traits.

What of the child involved with drug experimentation or regular use? The signs are often subtle and can be confused with normal adolescence. But when the signs continue to come up, you can be assured it's not an adolescent adjustment problem. It's alcohol or other drugs.

If we've heard it once, we've heard it a thousand times from shocked parents: "We had no idea Tracy was using drugs. Sure her lifestyle had changed, but we assumed it was typical teenage behavior." People who work with drug and alcohol addicts every day can see the problem so much more easily than parents, who seem to be the last to know. So sometimes it's good to get a second opinion.

A wonderful couple came to me (Jim) concerned about their daughter's drop in grades. They were afraid she had a learning disability. I asked general questions about the girl's behavior, and after hearing their answers, I said, "I don't want to dismiss the possibility of a learning disorder, but I would bet my life's savings (not much on a youth minister's salary!) your daughter has a drug or alcohol problem. The signs and symptoms all fall into place."

Both parents stood up, thanked me for my time, and informed me I was absolutely wrong. Two months later, their daughter entered treatment for acute alcoholism.

Subtle Symptoms of Chemical Abuse

The following symptoms could point to problems other than drug abuse. But they all indicate problems needing professional treatment. If every symptom describes your child, immediate action should be taken. If only a few of the symptoms are present, they could be common aspects of the teenage years. But, we suggest you at least discuss your concerns with your child.

- secrecy
- change in friends
- change in dress and appearance
- increased isolation
- change in interests or activities
- drop in grades
- getting fired from an after-school job
- changes in behavior around the home
- staying out all night
- possession of a bottle of eye drops (to counter bloodshot eyes)
- dropping out of sports participation

Not-So-Subtle Symptoms

The following symptoms indicate chemical abuse. If several of these symptoms are present in your child, you should take action immediately before the problem develops into addiction.

- deep depressions accompanied by hours of extra sleep
- depression
- extreme withdrawal from the family
- increased, unexplained absenteeism from school
- little or no involvement in church activities
- increase in mysterious phone calls that produce a frantic reaction
- starting smoking
- money problems
- extreme weight loss or gain
- appearance of new friends, older than your child
- expulsion from school
- rebellious and argumentative behavior
- listening to heavy metal rock music with pro-drug songs
- acting disconnected or "spacey"
- physically hurting younger siblings
- attempting to change the subject or skirt the issue when asked about drug or alcohol use
- changing the word "party" from a noun to a verb
- discussing times in the future when he or she will be allowed to drink legally
- long periods of time in the bathroom
- burnt holes in clothes and furniture

Sure-Fire Indicators

When the following signs show up, there should be no question in your mind that your child is abusing drugs or alcohol. These are signals that the problem hasn't just started but has existed for some time. You will see only the tip of the iceberg. Most of the problem and its symptoms have been carefully hidden away so you don't intervene. But intervene is what you must do if these symptoms surface.

- paraphernalia found in the bedroom: strange vials, small bags, mirrors, pipes, tubes, razor blades, cigarette papers, foil, butane lighters, scales, matches
- possession of large amounts of money (indicates your child doesn't just use but is probably selling to other kids as well)
- needle marks on the arms, or clothing that prevents you from seeing the arms
- valuables disappearing from the house
- arrests due to alcohol- or drug-related incidents
- repeatedly bloodshot eyes
- dilated or pin-point pupils
- puffy or droopy eyelids that partially hang over the iris
- mention of suicide or an attempt at suicide
- disappearance or dilution of bottles in the liquor cabinet
- time spent with people you know use drugs and drink
- medicine disappearing from the medicine cabinet
- defending peers' right to use drugs or alcohol

Several problems other than chemical abuse can produce similar symptoms. An anorexic or deeply depressed person could have some of the signs. But if these symptoms are present, you need to act now. Intervention is required. Don't let the symptoms mount. Don't assume your child is just going through a stage.

As your suspicions mount, your child's awareness of those suspicions will also mount. So delay does no good. Discuss the problem with your spouse, seek professional help, and develop a plan of action. The worst thing you can do is react quickly in anger. Contain yourself until you've sought professional help to plan an intervention that is best for your child.

Drug Tests

When Sandy and I (Steve) go to a doctor, no matter what our reason for being there, the doctor usually takes a urine sample and performs other minor tests to pick up any problem he might not otherwise spot. I never had a doctor do that before Dr. Baylor. But he gave me an idea for a great way parents and their physicians can monitor kids' use of drugs.

If you have teenagers, it's a good idea to take them to the doctor at least twice a year for a check-up. And when you do, make it a standard procedure that your doctor request a urine sample. Then be sure the doctor does a drug test. Tell your kids ahead of time that the doctor runs drug tests on adolescents. That way they'll see it isn't just you but also the doctor who is insuring there's no drug problem.

If this is done from an early age, it won't cause conflict between you and your children. And if you actually suspect drug use, you can have the doctor perform a more extensive test.

Drugs are a terrible problem, and fighting them requires some extreme measures. Having a urine screen performed is a simple way for you to learn if your kids are in trouble. It also provides a way out for children faced with pressure to use drugs. They can tell their friends that their parents will find out because the doctor tests their urine.

Reactions

Because of your love for your children and the natural urge to deny problems, you may have difficulty dealing with a drug or alcohol problem if it does occur. You may even have become codependent, making denial and compensation a part of your life-style. By comparing your life to the symptoms of codependency listed below, perhaps you can determine whether your behavior fits the pattern of others who deny their loved one's problem or enable it to continue. If you see yourself in these descriptions, you need to seek professional help for yourself as well as your kids.

- Trying to cover up children's irresponsible behavior rather than discuss it openly with a spouse, school personnel, or a friend.
- Feeling that no matter how hard you try, you can do nothing to change your children's behavior.
- Spending an inordinate amount of time talking to your children about problems and pleading for change.
- Always questioning what you do and say, thinking that if you change, your kids might be motivated to change.
- Giving money to your kids behind your spouse's back.
- Spending a large part of your day worrying about the kids and their problems.
- Regularly sacrificing for your children, always putting their needs before your own.
- Feeling a growing need to control the behavior of your kids. (Rather than release them to greater independence, out of fear, you feel yourself wanting to hold on tighter and tighter.)

If you can't see the problem in your children, perhaps you can see yourself in the pattern of codependency. If so, you aren't alone. Millions of parents do all the wrong things for the right reasons. Love is powerful, especially for a child. But that love can be blind to your child's need for help, allowing the chemical addiction to progress. If you find yourself enabling the problem rather than stopping it, help is available. Getting that help for yourself is the best step in moving toward an ultimate solution. When you stop enabling, you're ready to intervene and save your kids' lives.

One of the most effective ways to identify drug and alcohol abuse is with what professionals call an assessment. We have included below an assessment tool for your use.

Questions for Parents[1]

You may suspect your children are having trouble with alcohol or other drugs, but short of smelling liquor on their breath or discovering pills in their pockets, how can you tell for sure? While symptoms vary, there are some common tip-offs. Your answers to the following questions will help you determine if a problem exists.

1. Have your children's personalities changed markedly? Do they change moods quickly, seem sullen, withdraw from the family, display sudden anger or depression, or spend hours alone in their rooms?
   Yes ☐   No ☐   Uncertain ☐
2. Have your kids lost interest in school, school activities, or school athletics? Have their grades dropped at all?
   Yes ☐   No ☐   Uncertain ☐
3. Have your children stopped spending time with old friends? Are they now spending time with kids who worry you? Are they secretive or evasive about who their friends are, where they go, and what they do?
   Yes ☐   No ☐   Uncertain ☐
4. Are you missing money or other objects from around the house (money needed for alcohol and drugs), or have you noticed that your children have more money (possibly from

selling drugs) than you would expect?

Yes □ No □ Uncertain □

5. Have your kids tangled with the law in a situation involving drugs in any way? (You can be sure that if this has happened, there have been other times—probably many—when they've been drinking or using drugs but haven't been caught.)

Yes □ No □ Uncertain □

6. Do your children get angry and defensive when you talk about alcohol and drugs, or do they refuse to discuss the topic at all? (People who are defensive about alcohol and drugs are often hiding how much they use.)

Yes □ No □ Uncertain □

7. Do you feel you're not getting straight answers about your children's whereabouts, activities, or companions? (A young person may also lie about matters that seem unrelated to alcohol or drugs.)

Yes □ No □ Uncertain □

8. Have you smelled alcohol on your kids' breath? Have you smelled marijuana on their clothing or in their rooms? Slurred speech, unclear thinking, swaggering gait, bloodshot eyes, dilated pupils, and imprecise eye movement may also be indicators.

Yes □ No □ Uncertain □

9. Have your children lost interest in previously important hobbies, sports, or other activities? Have they lost motivation, enthusiasm, and vitality?

Yes □ No □ Uncertain □

10. Have you ever found a hidden bottle, beer cans left in the car, marijuana seeds, marijuana cigarettes, cigarette rolling papers, drug paraphernalia (pipes, roach clips, stash cans,

etc.), capsules, or tablets?
Yes ☐ No ☐ Uncertain ☐

11. Have your children's relationships with you or other family
members deteriorated? Do your kids avoid family gatherings? Are they less interested in siblings, or do they now
verbally (or even physically) abuse younger siblings?
Yes ☐ No ☐ Uncertain ☐

12. Have your children ever been caught with alcohol or other
drugs at school or school activities?
Yes ☐ No ☐ Uncertain ☐

13. Have your kids seemed sick, fatigued, or grumpy (possibly
hung over) in the morning after drug or alcohol use was
possible the night before?
Yes ☐ No ☐ Uncertain ☐

14. Has your children's grooming deteriorated? Do they dress
in a way associated with drug or alcohol use? Do they seem
unusually interested in drug- or alcohol-related slogans,
posters, music, or clothes?
Yes ☐ No ☐ Uncertain ☐

15. Has their physical appearance changed? Do they seem
unhealthy, lethargic, more forgetful, or have a shorter attention span than before?
Yes ☐ No ☐ Uncertain ☐

This questionnaire is not a scientific instrument and is not meant
to definitively diagnose chemical abuse problems. Rather, the questions are "red flag" indicators, and your answers may show a need
for further action. Keep in mind that "yes" answers to some of these
questions may reflect normal adolescent behavior. Affirmative
answers to questions directly relating to alcohol and drug use (5, 8,
10, and 12) are, of course, special cause for concern; they indicate your

children are almost certainly abusing chemicals, and action should be taken.

In general, you should look for an emerging pattern. A couple of "yes" or "uncertain" answers should alert you to suspect alcohol and drug use, monitor the children more closely, talk to knowledgeable sources, and prepare to seek help.

If you answered yes to three or more questions, help is probably needed now. Your children may be in the experimental stages, if not heavily involved. Remember, it is very difficult to handle this problem without the help of professionals. This is not usually a problem that passes with time; it may well be a life-or-death matter. If you're concerned, take action: call a knowledgeable source such as your school counselor, other drug counselors who deal with adolescents, your local council on alcoholism, or another drug-alcohol agency, and discuss this questionnaire.

Student Information

Most young people have used alcohol in one form or another, but few recognize alcoholism as a disease that can affect the young as well as the old. Ask your children to take the following short test; it may tell them something about themselves.

Yes No
☐ ☐   1. Do you lose time from school due to drinking?
☐ ☐   2. Is it necessary for you to drink to have fun?
☐ ☐   3. Do you drink to build up your self-confidence?
☐ ☐   4. Do you drink alone?
☐ ☐   5. Is drinking affecting your reputation—or do you care?
☐ ☐   6. Do you drink to escape from school or home worries?
☐ ☐   7. Do you feel guilty after drinking?

Yes	No	
☐	☐	8. Does it bother you if someone says you drink too much?
☐	☐	9. Do you sneak drinks from your parents' supply or anyone else's?
☐	☐	10. Do you generally "make out" better when you drink?
☐	☐	11. Do you get into financial troubles by buying liquor?
☐	☐	12. Do you feel a sense of power when you drink?
☐	☐	13. Have you lost friends since you've started drinking?
☐	☐	14. Have you started hanging around with kids who drink?
☐	☐	15. Do most of your friends drink less than you?
☐	☐	16. Do you drink until you're drunk or the bottle is empty?
☐	☐	17. Have you ever had a complete loss of memory from drinking?
☐	☐	18. Have you ever been to a hospital or arrested for drunk driving or being drunk in public or at school?
☐	☐	19. Do you turn off to any studies or lectures about drinking?
☐	☐	20. Do you think you may have a problem with liquor?

__   __   TOTALS

If you answered yes to any one question, it could be a warning that you're becoming a problem drinker. If you answered yes to any two questions, you might already be a problem drinker. If you answered yes to any three questions, you probably are a problem drinker.

CHAPTER NINE

Learning to Intervene

New Life Treatment Centers, Inc. advertises on many Christian radio programs. As a result, it receives phone calls from people with a variety of religious convictions. These callers want help because they or someone they love has reached a point of crisis. They call ready to take action, yet they often fail to act because they hold beliefs that prevent finding a solution. In fact, we're amazed how some people use Christianity to avoid taking responsibility.

One day a lady called who desperately needed to read Dr. James Dobson's book *Love Must Be Tough.* (She also needed a good dose of common sense.) She believed you could sit back and love anyone into changing. Concerned about her alcoholic husband and drug-using son, she wanted to know how to pray better to bring about change.

The phone counselor recommended she do an intervention on both of them to motivate them to get help. She was unwilling. It would show a lack of faith, she said; it wouldn't be the Christian thing to do. We don't think she fully understood Christianity.

The New Testament tells of a gentle and loving Christ who came to a point He finally had enough and performed the first intervention in recorded history. We know He greatly loved the money changers in the temple, as He loves all human beings. His love finally brought Him to a point of being unwilling to watch them continue in their destructive behaviors. So He overturned their tables and threw them out. Very quickly they felt the consequences of their behavior (cf. Matt. 21:12,13).

Just like Christ, we sometimes must make the tough decision to stop someone from moving down a path of destruction. We must intervene. We must love a person so much that we act on his or her behalf, even if acting is painful.

Long before an intervention is necessary, parents should teach their children about alcohol and drugs, beginning as early as elementary school. The education should be backed up by training that involves increasing rewards for responsible behavior and increasing restrictions for irresponsible acts. Then parents need to know how to identify the use of alcohol and drugs, focusing on peers, appearance, and behavior.

If you detect chemical abuse by your children, the next step is to intervene so the addiction does not progress one day longer than it has to. This chapter is designed to help you understand the intervention process and how that process can assist in changing your kids' behavior. Because of interventions, thousands of people have been spared their lives, families, careers, and, especially in the case of adolescents, their futures.

Kids in Denial

Once you identify that your child has a drug or alcohol problem, as a responsible parent, you must not only break through your own denial but also help your child with his or her refusal to see the problem. Keep in mind that your child's denial will be stronger than yours. Whatever your child admits to is the mere tip of the iceberg. Multiply what you know of the problem by five, and you'll be closer to how serious the situation is.

Once confronted, your child will deny the accusations to protect what he or she has come to depend on. Do not listen to the minimization and rationalization. The intervention process is a powerful tool that can break through your kid's denial.

Hitting Bottom

Kids, just like adults, will use drugs and alcohol until they hit bottom. For years, those working with alcoholics and drug addicts believed people had to hit bottom on their own. You would hear statements like, "That guy has a lot more drinking to do before anyone can help him." The theory was that everyone should sit around and watch an addict lose family, friends, money, job, freedom, and everything else, then come to the realization that the only way to go is up. Recovery doesn't have to begin under those circumstances.

Sometimes a crisis or tragedy, especially a life-threatening tragedy, can break the cycle. Some stop using when they're in an automobile accident and are almost killed or lose a limb. The glimmer of death motivates them to reach out for help. For others, a drug overdose leaves them just this side of death, and they recover from the drugs intent on never using again. Seeing a friend die or come close to death is tragedy enough to change the course of drug usage for some. But no one should wait for an unforeseen crisis or tragedy to effect change in the life of a child. That has happened too often, resulting in needless handicaps and losses of life.

All the horrible consequences of out-of-control addiction can be avoided through the process of intervention. This process helps people face the reality of the drug or alcohol problem, hit bottom in a controlled environment, and begin recovery. Forcing children to hit bottom early raises their level of "bottom," enabling them to recover with much more of life intact. Intervention nearly always changes the addict for the better, and it always changes the family for good.

Intervention Process

The intervention process refers to a series of actions taken by the family that will lead to change in the addict. Since most change is brought about by crisis, intervention precipitates a crisis. It brings the full weight and pain of the addictive behavior onto the person. Just as soothing family pain prevents recovery, so turning up the volume on the pain forces needed changes. In doing these things, a stable but miserable situation is disrupted, making room for growth. Here's what an intervention process looks like:

Assessment. When a family decides to intervene with a child, the first step is an assessment of the family by a professional. The assessment is designed to determine several things, including the family's strength. If the family has been living on eggshells for some time and family members are involved in destructive behavior, they may be too weak to be effective. The parents may need counseling to strengthen themselves before they can help in the intervention process.

The other reason for the assessment is to determine whether other members of the family are chemically dependent. Many interventions have been destroyed when the addict pointed out that his or her substance abuse was no worse than that of someone else in the family. Parents need to treat their own chemical dependencies first.

If there is no chemical dependency among other family members, if there's adequate strength to perform the intervention, and if addiction is verified in the child, the counselor will recommend that the process continue.

Classes. The family must then attend classes to become familiar with addiction, codependency, and intervention. These classes are offered through most drug treatment facilities. Some counselors specialize in the intervention process. You'll be able to find classes with just a few phone calls.

Family members need to hear a lecture on how addiction progresses and follows a predictable path leading either to death, insanity, or recovery. They will be given reading assignments to reinforce that others have also had children trapped in addiction. They learn, too, about the enabling process and how everyone in the family has sheltered the addict from the consequences of his or her behavior.

As they learn about enabling and other destructive roles, their behavior toward the addict begins to change. That's why many interventions never occur; the addict senses that something is happening and may volunteer for treatment before the event can take place. The last information the family learns is how to conduct an intervention, including how to accumulate data that can be used effectively in the intervention.

Intervention rehearsal. After the classes are presented, the family conducts an intervention rehearsal. They go through what they will say as the counselor acts out what the addict is likely to do in reaction. They practice instructing the addict on which alternatives are acceptable and which are not. For instance, the family determines that maintaining the status quo is not acceptable, and they decide what form of treatment would be best for the child. When the intervention is adequately rehearsed, the family and counselor set a date for the event.

Intervention data. The data for the intervention are carefully collected so as to help the addict see the need for help. The data must conform to the following guidelines:

1. They must be related to the drinking or drug-taking behavior, or to events actually witnessed.
2. They must include consumption levels and consequences. For example: "Ted, you drank two bottles of wine and stuffed them under your bed. That night you got out of bed, fell down the stairs, and broke your wrist."
3. They must include the date and time the drinking or drugging occurred.
4. They must always be presented with care and concern.
5. They must include feelings related to the drinking and drugging events.
6. They must point out the contradictions and conflicts in values and behaviors.
7. They must acknowledge attempts to control, quit, or change behavior.

When all the data adhere to these guidelines, they are very effective in helping the addict face reality.

Intervention alternatives. The family must be in agreement on acceptable and unacceptable alternatives for the addict. The primary alternative is for the addict to seek professional help from a quality treatment center. If the addict refuses that, a secondary alternative is spelled out: perhaps going to an Alcoholics Anonymous meeting each week, stopping drinking, and obtaining help from addiction specialists.

Sometimes an addict simply cannot be moved to seek help, and then the "what if" clause must be used. It lays out a predetermined course of action if the drinking or drugging happens again. This would include agreeing to obtain intensive treatment or leaving the house if help continues to be rejected. The family should also plan alternatives for themselves, such as separation, family therapy, or involvement in a support group. These are not presented as threats, but as choices for the long-term good of the family.

Intervention event. The event is a therapeutic session in which the addict is confronted with data concerning specific situations, how he or she made family members feel, and what the family wants the addict to do. The entire session is designed to motivate the person to get help. In a typical intervention, the counselor asks the addict to commit to staying in the session for at least one hour. The addict is told that everyone in the room is there because he or she cares and wants to discuss some information.

When the commitment is obtained, the session begins. The individuals then take turns presenting information, the data, while the addict listens. Each person relates two or three events, his or her reactions and feelings. When everyone is done, the alternatives are presented, and the addict is asked to get help. If the person does not agree to get help, the contingency plan is enacted, and the addict might be asked to leave home until he or she is willing to seek help. That rarely happens, however, because the person almost always agrees. But whatever the outcome, the addict's behavior will never be the same. The game is over, because the family has become wise to the progression of the problem and is resolved not to let it continue unchallenged.

Why Intervention Works

After months or years of unsuccessfully trying everything to stop a chemical abuse problem, some people find it hard to believe that intervention produces change in almost every case. But it does, and there are clear reasons why it's so effective.

First, a professional is in charge. The addict is not responding to the emotional strains that exist between family members. The counselor has the most direct interaction with the addict and maintains control over the session. With the professional in charge, there's little likelihood of the person storming out of the room in anger. The professional also prevents the session from becoming a shouting match, keeping everyone focused on the problem and what needs to be done, stopping any attempts to disrupt the process.

During the intervention training process, family members have had a chance to work through some of their anger and resentment resulting from the drug or alcohol abuse. So they come to the intervention with their emotions in check. Their lack of hostility is mirrored by the addict. The person's defensiveness is greatly reduced when he or she senses this is not a yelling, blaming, or condemning session.

The realization of the family's concern helps produce the needed result. As family members give information to the addict, he or she can't help but hear and feel the support in their voices. Perhaps for the first time in years, the addict hears the family speak without judging or criticizing. That change has a powerful impact: the addict knows something is different and something must change.

All the information presented is related to out-of-control behavior, so the addict doesn't feel personally attacked. The person hears about recent events, all involving drugs or alcohol, all involving negative consequences, and all causing the family uncomfortable emotions. This has a tremendous impact, because no one hints that the person is bad or inadequate. Rather, the problem has been documented and presented in such an objective form that it cannot be denied, while personal attacks have been completely left out.

Talking to a patient after an intervention had been performed on her, I (Steve) asked how she had felt during the process. She told me there was initial anger followed by relief. Then she made a most important statement: the intervention was the first time anyone had talked to her in a way she could hear. I believe that's because the intervention process takes away the need to be defensive.

The other factor making intervention successful is a clearly defined direction and goal for the session. The child is asked to see the reality of his or her drinking or drugging and then do something about it. Of course, almost everyone in that situation will say, "Okay, I'll stop forever. No, really, I mean it. You convinced me. I'll never touch the stuff again."

But intervention works beyond that, because the alternatives have been prearranged. The addict thinks he or she can get off the hook by admitting what the evidence has proved and saying it has changed his or her life. But once the admission is made, the alternatives of help and treatment are presented. That's when the full force of the intervention takes hold, because then each family member declares his or her love and a deep desire that the addict take advantage of the help that's already been arranged. Those tough-loving family members, committed to helping the person recover, produce the first step of hope in the life of the addict.

Intervention isn't easy, because the addiction to alcohol and drugs is so powerful. It isn't the ultimate solution and never happens exactly according to plan. Nor is it the intervention alone that causes needed changes in the family. The decision by the parents to intervene is the beginning of the change process. And, because denial is so strong and recurring, some form of intervention will have to happen over and over. Until the addict has taken full responsibility for his or her actions and recovery, every day can be another small intervention, moving the person toward recovery.

Intervention has helped tens of thousands of addicts. In recent years, Betty Ford has been among many well-known people who sought help. And the vast majority of interventions produce a recovering person who goes on to motivate others toward recovery. Imagine how many people Mrs. Ford has helped because of the intervention conducted by her family. Imagine how many people your children may affect after you intervene and lead them toward recovery. Each intervention can save a life; sometimes, it can save hundreds.

CHAPTER TEN

Obtaining Treatment

Ronnie convinced his parents that the small pouch of cocaine they found in his room was a remnant of a past life; the drugs were there only because he forgot to throw them out. He persuaded them to help him start a new life. All he needed was a car and he could find work. They agreed to the plan and purchased the car, stipulating that he had to make the payments from the money he earned. He turned the agreement into an opportunity for gain through manipulation. For about the hundredth time, his parents had taken the bait.

The tragedy occurred only three days after the new car was first parked in the driveway. First, the assistant principal called from the high school to ask where Ronnie was. A random check had uncovered Ronnie's truancy. But that was just the beginning. The next call came from a police officer who informed Ronnie's parents that he had been involved in a crash while driving under the influence of alcohol. He had been taken to a hospital with a concussion. At the hospital, his mother was given the number of a treatment center.

By the time I (Steve) saw him, Ronnie was ready to begin a new life, and he did. His parents by his side, he started over with the help of a treatment team that gave him tools to stay sober. Not everyone uses the tools, but Ronnie did and still does.

If your children have been identified as having alcohol or drug problems, you want the professional help that will benefit them the most. You must fight back the urge to handle the problem alone. Drug addiction and alcoholism are powerful forces that cannot be fought alone. In Proverbs 20:18, the wise person is urged to seek good counsel when waging war. That's what you must do if you're going to win.

This chapter is meant to help you make wise decisions about the type of help you obtain for your kids. It's important to note that all programs and counselors are not the same. Some have very different values and beliefs from yours. Knowing that, many people make no decisions because they're afraid of throwing their children to the wolves. Their fear is valid, but their action is not. The guidelines presented here will enable you to find help with the confidence that your children will be strengthened and your values supported.

When Does a Person Need Professional Help?

Most people seek professional help much later than they should. They wish for the best or think problems will get better: after the holidays, when work pressure subsides, after graduation. Unfortunately, with drug and alcohol abuse, things usually get worse before they get better.

The natural tendency is to try to handle all our problems ourselves, even our children's chemical abuse. But if everything you've tried has failed, it's time to get help. That's not a sign of weakness but of strength and love.

Some people advocate doing as little as possible for as long as possible. But this can cause failure or at the least waste time. You need to put every force available to work on the problem, treating it like a spreading cancer that must be cut out immediately. Any extra time and money will be well spent if it produces the recovery you desire. Are you willing to do whatever it takes to help your child recover, to go the extra mile rather than choose what appears to be the easiest path?

Chemical abuse affects every area of a person's life. The mind won't work properly, having been saturated with chemicals. The body will likewise be chemically imbalanced. And the soul of a person, along with values and beliefs, becomes damaged. For an addict to recover, each area must be treated. That's why professional care is needed. No one individual can treat the totality of a person experiencing the severe problems associated with drug addiction or alcoholism.

Many addicts have recovered on their own through attending a group. But many have walked away after one meeting and felt it wasn't for them. Many have prayed, been immediately delivered from their addiction, and gone years without a drink or a drug. Others have made an instantaneous, miraculous recovery, only to start drinking again a few months later. And many more have been praying for years and have not changed at all. It's easy to focus on the quick and convenient method. It's especially easy if that appears to be the more spiritual approach. But too many failures exist for any one approach to this complex problem. Obtaining professional help brings together a variety of disciplines to help you win the battle for your children.

In some cases, the need for professional help is obvious, such as when medical attention is required. An addicted person going through withdrawal from drugs is an example. This is something a pastor or other counselor cannot treat alone. In extreme cases, it is actually possible for a person to suffer physical or neurological brain damage if a naive counselor doesn't seek medical advice.

The medical profession is equipped to handle these life-threatening problems. It's important that when help is sought, it's obtained from a resource that is intent on helping without destroying the supports that exist for that person.

Any quality helping professional or organization, whether a church, community resource program, or therapist, should know the best resources available. But sometimes these organizations haven't done the research yet, which means you'll have to do more. When you start your search for helpers, don't ask only about drug and alcohol addiction. Treatment should be holistic and include a positive approach to morals, family, and Christian beliefs. A well-balanced program focuses not only on the addiction but also takes into consideration the spiritual, mental, physical, and social aspects of life.

When a young person is clearly diagnosed as having an addiction, we are partial to a program that uses a treatment team rather than a single counselor or pastor. For example, when a young person is admitted to an inpatient program or outpatient clinic, a team of qualified and caring therapists, doctors, nurses, and other professionals combine their strengths to overpower the grip of addiction. Any one of these professionals acting separately would be unable to devote the time and energy needed. The staff must be willing to do whatever is required. But so must the patient. When patient, family, and treatment team are all willing to do whatever it takes for as long as necessary, there is tremendous hope for change.

While working in treatment in California, we saw many affluent parents who were unwilling to admit they couldn't help their children with alcohol and drug problems. They could manage large companies and major charities, so they felt they should be able to handle any problem that arose within the family. This attitude is similar to the tradition of old Texans: if the problem exists within your fence, it's your job to fix it. It's hard for parents to give up control and allow someone else to help them. But parents must reach that point if children are to recover.

When does a person need professional help? Usually now. If you've been asking that question, it's time to stop questioning and start acting.

Making a Good Choice the First Time

In every life, certain key moments usher in change and hope for a new beginning. Those moments are rare, however, so if someone in your family has come to the point of realizing the need for change and desires help, it's important that good decisions be made the first time around. It could be some time, or maybe never, before the opportunity or motivation to change will come again. You don't want to waste what could be the best chance for change.

Also, few people have unlimited resources to pay for treatment. Whether paying all the costs or just the deductible portion after insurance, your money should go toward the greatest hope for help. Most rely on insurance to cover the bulk of the expense, but many insurance companies limit the amount they will pay or the days they will cover a person in treatment. Those precious dollars must not be wasted on ineffective or inappropriate treatment.

More important than money or resources, of course, is the need for the person you love to be in a program that is constructive rather than destructive. Programs vary in their effectiveness, and some can do more harm than good. In some treatment centers, for example, poor supervision allows drug dealers and other patients to bring in drugs. That type of environment clearly is not good and can destroy any possibility for recovery.

In some programs, the problem can be drugs from a source other than drug dealers. For instance, some programs overutilize medication to control patients. This, combined with an unstructured program, can be a miserable experience for those being treated. They can become further trapped in their problems. Medication is not bad for all patients. Sometimes, although rarely, it's a necessity. But if it's used too frequently or liberally, the effect can be to move patients from one addiction to another.

Some programs have other counterproductive elements. Probably the most prevalent and the most serious are destructive attitudes and behaviors. When you go to a treatment center, for example, you might sense a mood of depression or high anxiety from both staff and patients. If a visitor can sense that in a short time, you can imagine how strong those feelings must be for the patients who are there twenty-four hours a day. The negative environment is created by unhealthy staff attitudes and behaviors, which are always reflected in the patients they treat. It's essential that a person seeking help for the first time secure it in a safe and healthy environment where staff are motivated to provide quality care.

Types of Programs

Numerous types of treatment programs exist. Each has its strengths and weaknesses. We have tried to list each type, along with a few comments. At the end of the book, we have provided a national resource phone number, managed by New Life Treatment Centers. When you call, the counselor can direct you to a local helping agency and help you determine the best type of treatment for your child and your situation.

Inpatient hospital. Inpatient treatment is conducted in a hospital with a full complement of medical staff, including doctors and nurses. They are assisted by a team of professionals who have training in social work, psychology, and counseling. This is the most comprehensive treatment available and keeps the patient in a protected environment during the initial phases. It is covered by most major insurances.

Residential treatment. Residential treatment is conducted outside a hospital and is much less expensive than inpatient care, although it is sometimes not covered by insurance. A person requiring medical attention would not do well in this setting. But someone without a medical crisis could find residential treatment an excellent alternative. The medical team is not as strong, though the program staff are usually skilled and experienced. Residential treatment also provides a protected environment and a time away from the family so that healthy adjustments can be made in family relationships.

Halfway house. A halfway house also provides a place for separation from the family and, to a lesser degree than the first two alternatives, a protected environment. Everyone in the house is recovering, and most residents attend school during the day. When they come home in the evening, residents attend counseling sessions and Alcoholics and Narcotics Anonymous meetings. For those who have had repeated relapse, this is an excellent option for long-term sobriety.

Day treatment. A strong day treatment program includes everything found in inpatient treatment, except that the patients go home at night. This is much less costly than inpatient care, but insurance is just beginning to cover some of these programs in a few locations. When separation from the home is required or a person cannot control the urge to use in the initial recovery stages, this would not be a good choice.

Outpatient care. For some, outpatient care is all that's needed. The person goes to a group meeting in the evening, after school or work. These programs must be highly structured to be successful, especially with kids who are not yet committed to recovery. Because the hours are fewer and the program less intensive, recovery can be a much more frustrating experience for the family if a relapse occurs. When that's the case, inpatient treatment should be pursued.

However, excellent outpatient help can be obtained through local Alcoholics Anonymous and Alateen chapters, group therapy, or private counseling. We are also encouraging churches and youth groups to start small, intensive, outpatient groups for kids with drug and alcohol problems.

Wrong Reasons for Choosing a Treatment Program

In the search for quality treatment, people are motivated by different events and pressures. At times, choosing a program becomes less than a totally objective decision. It's essential that you not make a selection based on the wrong reasons. Some common wrong reasons are listed below:

Newness of the facility. Whenever a new facility opens, public relations announcements and advertising herald the event, and it's easy to get caught up in the hype. The new program may be of the highest possible quality, but you won't know that from press releases and ads. Take the time to find other reasons to choose a program. Remember, the new kid on the block isn't necessarily the best kid.

Extracurricular activities and amenities. Some programs take patients horseback riding. There may be a swimming pool on the grounds. The staff may give patients the opportunity to play golf. But those things don't make people well; they make people's stay a little more comfortable. Often people need to feel discomfort before they become or stay motivated to change. If they're made too comfortable or are allowed too many diversions from dealing with their problems, treatment can become a waste of time. What makes a great program is the content, the schedule, the quality of the groups, and, most importantly, the competence of the staff.

Advertising. The thousands of advertisements on television and in newspapers and magazines help motivate people into treatment. But a treatment center should not be chosen based on an ad. Commercials are no indication of the level of care available, and many of the best treatment centers do little or no advertising.

The choice of the adolescent. When a child is in need of treatment, it's better to rely on your own judgment rather than the desires of the adolescent. An addict has little ability to make a rational decision about the best type of care. What kids do know is which treatment centers have a free flow of drugs. They also know where the drug culture and hard rock paraphernalia are allowed and where they're discouraged. Sometimes a child will want to go into a center because a girlfriend or boyfriend is there. But the last person you want choosing the treatment center is the one needing help.

A physician's reputation. A parent might see a well-respected doctor on television or hear that doctor on the radio. Because of the doctor's charisma or reputation, the parent might think that the treatment program with which the physician is associated must be good. But that's not necessarily true. Less than 5 percent of a patient's time will be spent with a physician. Treatment programs are designed so that the physician isn't the only person treating the patient. A team approach is used in many centers, and the team is much more important than any one member, including the physician.

Cost. Drug and alcohol problems are life-and-death matters. Cost should have little to do with where help is obtained. Often, inexpensive programs are without enough staff to meet patients' needs. Salaries may be so low that only entry-level people are used in the treatment process. It's much better to find the best treatment resource available and then find a way to finance the cost.

Proximity. If everything else were equal, the closer the unit, the better the opportunity would be for the entire family to receive treatment. And the more treatment the whole family receives, the greater the chance for total recovery. But fine programs make allowances for out-of-town families. Special tracks are designed to accommodate and treat the whole family so that distance isn't as major a factor in recovery. Don't make convenience the biggest part of your decision.

Community image of the hospital. A hospital may have a strong reputation that covers up a weak alcohol and drug treatment program. The image of a hospital or the amount of its community service involvement should not be used to measure a treatment program. The unit is only a portion of the hospital, and all that matters is what goes on in that unit. Horrible acute care hospitals can have wonderfully healthy drug and alcohol units, because the two services are often managed by separate organizations.

Correct Reasons for Choosing a Treatment Center

The following reasons are the correct ones for choosing a treatment center and offer the best hope for obtaining effective help:

A well-maintained facility. The first indication of a commitment to quality care is a facility that is clean and well-maintained. It doesn't have to be the newest or the biggest or the nicest hospital. But your confidence in the program should be strengthened by the outside appearance and interior maintenance. If the facility is not clean and appears run-down, it's obvious the patients' comfort is not a high priority. But where you find a commitment to the structure of a building, you often find quality care.

A referral by someone you trust. With so many resources to choose from, it's always better to have a recommendation from someone you can trust, someone who has helped many people get help. Your pastor could be an excellent source of guidance if he has referred others and is pleased with the results of a particular program. Find several people who have had success, and ask how they did it.

A referral by someone who has been through the program. Nothing speaks louder than the successful treatment of a person and his or her long-term recovery. No one knows a program better than someone who has been treated there. If you don't know someone who has been through a program, you might ask the center for the name of a successful alumnus. That can help you determine whether the qualities of the program are likely to meet the needs of your family.

A strong team approach to treatment. Two basic types of programs exist in alcohol and drug treatment:

1. Weak staff, dominant physician. In these programs, the doctor makes all the decisions about patient care. The rest of the staff, who spend most of the time with the patient, are disregarded in planning the course of treatment. There have been times when a physician has recommended a pass for a patient who other staff members knew was suicidal. The resulting death could have been avoided if the physician had consulted the staff. A doctor with a strong ego and disregard for the opinions of other treatment staff can be a detriment to patient care.

2. Strong staff, physician as team member. In this environment, the nurses, therapists, patient, technicians, and doctor work together to form treatment plans that cover all the patient's needs. All staff members express their views about the patient before the treatment plan is developed. This is extremely important, since most programs have more than one physician involved with the treatment process.

Where a weak staff and a bullying physician team up, the treatment is poor, the care inconsistent, and the results less than satisfactory. Where a strong staff places high value on the effectiveness of the team, a greater chance for quality care occurs. And where this occurs, the staff are more satisfied with their jobs, and the teams stay together longer, providing consistent care over the years.

Healthy support for a sober life-style. This includes:

1. Music. Most programs allow patients to bring in tape recorders and radios and listen to any type of music they desire. Yet many

authorities are now saying heavy metal and hard rock music are not conducive to recovery. The music is full of references to drugs, death, rebellion, immoral sex, and other unhealthy behaviors. This sick music is an integral part of the drug culture and reinforces the patient's desire to use again. Where music is controlled, a healthier environment exists.

2. Movies. Viewing of movies that focus on violence, sex, and crude language is allowed in many units. This also is counterproductive to total life-style change. Filling the mind with examples of negative behavior does nothing but reinforce those forms of behavior. Quality care means monitoring what is viewed and providing positive alternatives.

3. Language. This is a clear indicator of a person's inner state of mind. Foul language should be discouraged. Good communication that is inoffensive to others helps a person fit into a civil and moral life-style.

4. View of sex. If staff members believe in the personal dignity of the individual, they will confront any behavior that is dishonorable or could cause another person to be degraded. Often kids will replace their dependency on drugs with a dependency on sexual pleasure. This behavior must be confronted as soon as it surfaces.

Personal attention. Poor programs will tell you that individual sessions are not important for quality care. That's because they have such low staff-to-patient ratios that no time exists for individual sessions. To determine whether a program really cares, you must find out if it offers individual therapy for all the patients on an almost-daily basis. If the staff-to-patient ratio is low, the quality of care will be low.

Family treatment. When one person becomes sick with an alcohol or drug problem, the entire family also gets sick. People do not deteriorate in a vacuum. It's important that each person in the family receive help if the patient is to be helped long-term. A healthy patient going back into an unhealthy family will only become unhealthy again.

We have often seen the person in treatment as the healthiest member of the family. As a sacrificial lamb, that person has allowed him or herself to be treated so that the whole family will get help. One young girl simply would not go home to her parents. She would relapse just before discharge, and treatment would begin again. Finally someone broke through to what was really going on. She was a victim of sexual abuse, and she didn't want to face those times without drugs. She knew the pain of abuse would lead her back to the chemicals. Her family had not been forced to participate in treatment, so this had not been detected before. For her to return to that sick family would have been futile. Her family needed treatment as badly as she did.

Staff attitudes of sensitivity and service. Any time a person enters treatment, pain, emotional turmoil, hours of preparation, and money have been expended. The family should expect a lot from the program. The staff should realize what the people have been through to arrive at treatment. Each person, especially the patient, should be approached with great sensitivity. Staff members should display an attitude of service in each encounter with the family.

Traditional values supported. When you or someone in your family goes into treatment, you should be assured that traditional values will not be undermined. Religious values should not be challenged but instead incorporated into the treatment process. Don't be afraid to ask about staff attitudes toward beliefs you and your family hold dear. If the program cannot support those beliefs, treatment could be counterproductive.

In particular, Christian parents should select a quality Christian program. Many centers talk of a spiritual dimension to treatment, but "spiritual" and "Christian" can be two very different things. Some programs, for example, take their patients to the desert for an experience that combines Indian folklore, astrology, and pantheism. Such an experience would be a Christian parent's nightmare. And since recovering addicts are at a point of change and strongly desire to learn a new way of life, they are impressionable and easily led astray. Prevent your children from focusing on the power of man or the gods of nonbelievers by seeking the best treatment in a Christian setting delivered by Christian professionals.

Components of Quality Care

It's difficult to describe what constitutes quality treatment. You can't just compile a list and say that if the items on the list are present, quality care is guaranteed. It's more complicated than that. Quality care is a process that occurs over time, with numerous people inter-acting and bringing their resources to bear on the patient. Some pro-grams are stronger in certain areas than others. Two programs could use radically different approaches and still provide quality treatment. But to assist you in finding quality care for someone in your family, common components can be identified.

As mentioned before, the facility does not have to be fancy or new, but it should be clean and well-maintained. Never leave a person at a facility you cannot be proud of.

The overall attitude of the staff must show love and concern. Harsh, angry staff produce harsh, angry patients.

The staff should have plenty of experience and excellent credentials. Low-paid, underqualified, and inexperienced staff cannot provide quality treatment.

A strong team approach should be used, because it means a patient will get the most appropriate care. Often a patient can fool one or two staff or remain in denial if few people give input into treatment. But when a team is at work, the patient is more likely to deal with reality.

Visits should be monitored closely. Treatment is a time to focus on change, not old friends. Often those who come to visit are people with whom the patient should not associate.

Television, music, reading material, dress, language, and attitude should all be supervised by the staff so that each patient contributes to a positive environment, allowing everyone the greatest chance to change.

The treatment provided should be a blend of group, individual and family therapy. Lectures, films, and discussion groups should fill a patient's day. There should be little time to sit and do nothing.

Family treatment must also be a priority. Putting a recovering patient back into a sick family makes relapse likely.

Never turn over someone in your family to a program that will undermine the spiritual foundation you have established.

Quality treatment addresses the whole person. The physical, mental, emotional, social and spiritual areas must all be considered.

The program should include attendance at some type of follow-up support group. This ongoing aftercare is the best insurance that all areas will continue to be addressed.

Whatever the cost, quality care must be the priority. Where it exists, patients get well. As mentioned before, there's no better indicator of the quality of a program than what has happened in the lives of those who received treatment.

Treatment is a great opportunity for an entire family to recover. If your children need help, do not delay in seeking professional assistance.

CHAPTER ELEVEN

Parents' Guide to Handling Relapse

For three years the McMillans tried to help their son. They took him out of one school and put him in another. They promised him a car and money for college. They pleaded and cajoled, but the situation grew worse each day. Finally they realized that only treatment could help their boy. His drug problem would not respond to home remedies.

They went to the Yellow Pages, looked under "Alcohol and Drug Treatment Centers," and made the call. For the first time in three years, they felt hope. The counselor guided them through the process of intervention, resulting in their son going into treatment.

The boy did well in the program. The therapists loved him and enjoyed having him in their groups. He was a leader among the other kids. He told everyone he really wanted to make a new start. And while there, he wrote letters to all his drug-using friends, telling them of his new, sober life. As he showed the letters to his parents, their hopes soared. The son they loved was theirs to enjoy again.

Three weeks after graduation from the program, the boy was

arrested for possession of methamphetamines. As the McMillans drove to the police station, the word "failure" summed up all their thoughts and emotions. They felt their son had failed. They felt they had failed. And they felt the treatment center had failed.

It was a common reaction to a common post-treatment event called "relapse." But relapse and failure are not synonymous. For most people in recovery, relapse becomes the first stage of true progress based on reality, not false expectations. That proved to be true for the McMillans. The boy's relapse was not the end of recovery but the real beginning. It forced him to see the need for a comprehensive recovery plan that went far beyond determination and motivation.

People hope treatment is a quick, once-and-for-all fix that will require no more struggle in the family. But treatment is the beginning of the fix, not the fix itself. At least 40 percent of those who obtain help will relapse within the first year. Relapse fully acquaints addicts with the reality of their situation. If your children have obtained treatment, you must be prepared for relapse.

When we first began working with alcoholics and drug addicts, we were intensely saddened whenever we heard of a relapse. We viewed each one as a failure. Then we saw wonderful things happen as a result of relapse. Real recovery often began on the other side. Families pulled together in the ways they should have when treatment ended.

Once a relapse happens, the patient and family often develop a workable recovery plan. Treatment does not end when a person graduates from a program or is discharged from a hospital. Such formal treatment only forms the foundation of a recovery process that should continue for the rest of the addict's life. Even if the treatment experience is negative or the foundation isn't as strong as it could be, recovery can be successful if the family supports a plan for ongoing sobriety. Of all the things that happen in a treatment program, the best is that the child and family leave with a recovery plan.

Good coaches prepare a team for the struggle ahead. They practice game-like situations so team members will be fully prepared. And good coaches develop a plan they will follow during the competition. But the best coaches always go a step further. They also prepare the team for setbacks so the players know what to do if the other team scores first. It's not a total shock, and a new part of the game plan is implemented.

That's what a good recovery plan should do, too. It prepares the recovering addict to succeed, but it also lays out the steps to take if relapse occurs. This chapter is designed to help you understand what a good recovery plan includes and how it's used in preventing relapse or bringing good out of relapse, should it occur.

Recovery and Relapse Protection Plan

A comprehensive plan for recovery will address every area of a person's life. The longer the recovery is maintained, the more the plan will improve the quality of life. One of the most often heard mistakes is that a recovery plan neglected one or more areas. That's why a well-balanced, holistic plan is a must. We've listed below the most important guidelines for each area of the recovery plan.

Physical. Recovering people tend to neglect the body and its special needs, but that makes recovery much more difficult. Three areas need to be addressed.

1. Nutrition. The body pays a heavy price for addiction. The tissues and organs are damaged by the toxicity of the drugs and the poor nutrition that accompanies addiction. Eating habits need to change to insure that the body can recover strength and rebuild damaged tissue. Without a balanced diet, the body will limp along. In addition, most recovery professionals recommend a vitamin and mineral supplement.

Nutrition is also important to help stabilize blood sugar levels. When these levels are increased through food and drink high in sugar, the subsequent drop in blood sugar causes a strong sense of craving, restlessness, and often depression. Stories abound of people who began binge eating on sugary foods like ice cream and relapsed within days.

I (Jim) know of a twenty-two-year-old who had been sober for two years. She had just broken up with her fiancé. Her relapse did not begin with a binge of drinking but with a binge of eating. She started consuming food high in sugar. At a party for her niece she was out of control, eating several helpings of cake and ice cream. Five hours later, when the sugar high wore off, she found alcohol and began drinking again.

The best diet is high in protein, such as fish and poultry, and complex carbohydrates found in fresh vegetables, pasta, and other foods made from grains. Protein-rich foods and fresh vegetables make up the best diet to reduce blood sugar variances. It also helps to eat smaller meals more frequently rather than three large meals a day that cause the blood sugar levels to surge and recede dramatically.

Many recovering people are able to adjust their food intake, but they fail in the area of beverages. They either load up on highly sugared soft drinks with plenty of caffeine, or they consume hundreds of cups of coffee filled with caffeine. With kids, of course, the soft-drink binge becomes the biggest sugar and caffeine problem.

Both sugar and caffeine produce a stimulating or even hyper effect, but it doesn't last. As the blood-sugar level drops, the sensation of craving reaches a peak. This can lead to a relapse as the craving becomes uncontrollable.

Regulating caffeine and sugar intake also strengthens the recovery process by keeping the addict from experiencing extreme emotional highs and lows. Besides, recovery means learning to live without chemicals of any kind, clean and sober. For years, alcoholics have recovered while smoking and drinking coffee. But today we better understand the harmful effects of nicotine and caffeine. Thus, the decision to avoid them is a quality issue: the purer the recovery, the higher the quality of recovery.

2. Exercise. Exercise offers tremendous recovery benefits. It's the most natural form of stimulation and relaxation, building up strength and stamina while burning off stress. It's a productive way to fill time and work off boredom rather than allow boredom to lead to relapse. It also provides a sense of accomplishment, builds self-esteem and increases body tone while decreasing body fat. Exercise can help bring a family back together, too. Running, jogging, tennis, volleyball, bicycling, swimming, and skiing all provide fun times for the family to mend. People in recovery often feel like a time bomb, ready to explode at any minute. Exercise is the best way to defuse that bomb.

3. Rest and relaxation. In addition to proper nutrition and exercise, the body needs good rest, especially in the early stages of recovery. An adolescent coming out of treatment is used to going to bed at ten or eleven o'clock, and this schedule should be maintained. A proper amount of rest prevents depression and irritability and eliminates extended periods of temptation. The sleep pattern should vary little, even on weekends.

Another helpful tool is for the addict to take scheduled breaks for relaxation. Stopping to refocus in the middle of a hectic schedule can prevent the buildup of stress that could trigger a relapse. The wise addict learns to recognize the extreme pressure situations and control them before they become so intense they cannot be controlled. Knowing when to leave a situation and find a quiet corner in a hall or restroom helps keep the body relaxed and the emotions steady.

Mental. What a person thinks forms the basis for many feelings. If a person is always thinking about the horrible realities of life instead of the wonderful possibilities, it's only natural to be depressed. A strong relapse protection plan exposes the addict to people and events that give positive material for growth and understanding. The apostle Paul put it this way: "Finally, brothers, whatever is true, whatever is noble, whatever is right, whatever is pure, whatever is lovely, whatever is admirable—if anything is excellent or praiseworthy— think about such things" (Phil. 4:8).

Every recovery plan for adolescents should include reading material on addiction and recovery designed especially for kids. This will help them stay focused on the successful recoveries of others and the guidelines leading to long-term sobriety. In the recovering community, hundreds of tapes are filled with stories of success. Acquire those tapes, and during tough times, review those that are most helpful.

The key to focusing the mind in a positive manner, however, is attending live lectures and meetings, such as Alcoholics Anonymous or Narcotics Anonymous. Coming face to face with fellow strugglers in a large group helps to keep the thought process on track. Hearing other people's recovery stories, full of struggle and hope, adds new insight. It also prevents isolation. Be sure your children are scheduled to hear some good speakers and lectures, and find seminars that you can attend together.

Addicts need to experience new and powerful information about recovery. This is different from therapy where emotions are shared and processed. If a child leaves treatment and only goes to group therapy, the mental part of recovery will be neglected. So much negative input occurs at school and after school that life becomes discouraging. It's easy for a teenager's thinking to become confused about drugs and recovery. If you don't plan to counter those negative messages, they'll have a powerful impact that could subvert the entire recovery process. So guide addicts to places where healthy thinking can be reinforced.

We tell kids the age-old adage, "Garbage in, garbage out." If they put garbage into their minds, garbage will come out. However, if they put good thoughts into their minds, good will come out.

A young man went to a psychologist for help. He was experiencing the same dream every night. He told the counselor, "Every night a black cat and a white cat fight until one of them wins."

The psychologist asked, "Which one wins, the white one or the black?"

The young man replied, "Whichever one I feed the most."

We must teach young people that what they put in their minds will play a major role in how well they recover.

We challenge young people to consider reading through the New Testament or even the entire Bible in one year. It's incredible what the wisdom of the Bible can do. "For, 'All men are like grass, and all their glory is like the flowers of the field; the grass withers and the flowers fall, but the word of the Lord stands forever' " (1 Peter 1:24-25).

Emotional. Getting the proper nutrition, exercise, and mental input gives the emotions a greater chance of being steady and strong, able to avoid the dangerous extremes that trigger relapse. But emotional health also requires group sessions where feelings can be explored and expressed. Emotional recovery does not happen in isolation. Recovering adolescents must stay connected to others who are recovering and share with them their emotional ups and downs.

Recovering people often say they stopped growing up when they started drinking or using drugs. Many still feel emotionally like children at age thirty or forty. Give your kids experiences at home and in groups of recovering people where feelings can be identified, expressed, and managed. The goal is to help them mature into people who can handle emotional trauma without turning back to alcohol or drugs.

Social. As we've emphasized elsewhere, the social pressures on adolescents are extremely strong and difficult to counter. Alcoholics Anonymous talks about "changing playmates and playgrounds." For the alcoholic to recover, his choice of friends and hangouts must change. This is even more true for adolescents. As mentioned earlier, the clearest indicator your children use drugs is that they have friends who are known drug users. The clearest indicator of relapse is that your kids are associating with known drinkers and drug abusers.

Old drug-using friends must be replaced with "clean kids" and, whenever possible, with church groups. If children hang on to past acquaintances, it's evidence that treatment did little to adjust their life-styles. If that's the case, you may have to limit access to certain friends. Total restriction from a person is rarely helpful. It makes the attraction stronger in many instances. But you don't have to allow your children to be out with someone until 3 A.M. or be with that person every night of the week. When children cannot control themselves, you must assume more control.

One of the best ways to counter negative social experiences is to provide positive alternatives as a family. Encourage your children to invite other kids over for dinner. Plan weekend trips to the lake or beach and have your children's friends come along. If a concert is coming to town, plan to take your children with their friends. Be creative, and teach your children to create situations that will be supportive of a sober life-style.

Spiritual. Recovery is first and foremost a spiritual process. It's a journey out of the pleasures of the physical world and into the joys of spiritual life. Yet few people understand the importance of spiritual growth as a vital element of recovery.

Any person coming into recovery brings the weight of responsibility for a damaged past and guilt over the pain he or she has caused others. In spiritual recovery, the guilt, shame, and remorse are resolved. If they're not, it will be only a short time before the pain of guilt wears away the resistance to drink and take drugs. The recovery process will be shallow, a form of coping rather than a way to live abundantly, full of God's love. Each successful recovery, on the other hand, is established with a full understanding of a loving and forgiving God whose Son paid the price for our guilt.

Spiritual recovery isn't just for resolving the past, however. It also helps people find a purpose in life beyond material gain or recognition by others. Spiritual growth leads them to discover a life's mission beyond vocation.

Just because someone acknowledges God does not mean the person has achieved spiritual recovery. It's more comprehensive than that. To grow spiritually, each day must be turned over to and directed by God. Knowledge of Him needs to develop through worship, fellowship, Bible study, and prayer. Without those ingredients, spiritual growth is weak. We believe the "higher power" of the twelve-step program is not some obscure concept but the God of the Bible, and people can actually have a relationship with their "higher power" through Jesus Christ.

As a parent, you can set the pattern for spiritual growth. Through your own prayer life, Bible study, and church attendance, you can lead the way. Don't expect your children to grow spiritually if you aren't in the process of growing. If you want to see a miraculous transformation in your children, lead the way down the path of spiritual recovery.

Sample Recovery and Relapse Protection Plan

Before an addict graduates from treatment, it's essential that a recovery and relapse prevention plan be developed. It should address each of the five dimensions just discussed. It should also have a contingency plan to follow, if and when the original plan is abandoned or relapse occurs. The following is an example of what a recovery plan could look like.

Relapse Protection and Recovery Plan

To have a full and meaningful recovery, I will do the following things to help maintain my sobriety one day at a time (Jesus said, "Live one day at a time" [Matt. 6:34, TLB].):

Physical

1. Jog twenty minutes each afternoon after school.

2. Stay away from soft drinks and desserts except for desserts after special meals.

3. Take two breaks each day when stress builds up.

4. Eat chicken, fish, or meat and fresh vegetables every day, along with a vitamin and mineral supplement.

Mental

1. Attend one lecture on recovery at a treatment center each month.

2. Listen to at least one tape on recovery each week and write a paragraph about one important point from it.

3. Attend at least one speaker meeting a week.

4. Read a passage from *The Big Book of Alcoholics Anonymous* and some other book about recovery every day.

5. Read the Bible daily.

Emotional

1. Attend at least two discussion groups a week.

2. Continue to see a counselor until anger is worked out.

3. Write in a journal each day about struggles and new challenges.

4. Attend one aftercare group a week.

Social

1. Create a list of people who are a negative influence and commit to spending little time with them.

2. Create a list of people who are healthy influences and commit to spending a lot of time with them.

3. Go on at least one family outing a month that I plan.

4. Participate in church group activities.

Spiritual

1. Read the Bible every day.

2. Pray each day that God will use me and help me find a mission in life.

3. Attend church each Sunday I am in town and not sick.

4. Listen to at least one tape a month on spiritual recovery.

The following should take place if I fail to follow the recovery plan:

1. Phone my counselor for treatment and set up an appointment to discuss any problems or discouragements I might be having.

2. If this talk does not change my behavior and attitude, I will return to treatment before I use again. Treatment may be in the form of seeing an addiction specialist, attending an outpatient program, or going into a hospital.

3. If I am picked up by the police for an alcohol- or drug-related offense, my parents will assume I am guilty and not bail me out of jail or spend money for me to plead innocent. I understand they will allow me to experience the full weight of the consequences of my behavior.

_____

Signed

_____

Date

I (Steve) once worked with a beautiful young girl on her plan for recovery. Nothing was left uncovered. She was ready for a new life. There was just one problem. She went home and put her plan in the drawer and never looked at it again. Her parents also neglected to hold her accountable. Naturally she relapsed and was full of guilt and shame when she returned to treatment. If your children obtain treatment and develop recovery plans, be sure to hold them accountable. It's one of the best assurances for a strong recovery.

Relapse Indicators

The first indicator of relapse is *not* your child becoming stoned or drunk again. Other signs and symptoms are expressed long before then. If you see them, you can intervene at the beginning of the relapse progression, before the total relapse occurs.

The relapse progression starts with complacency. People in relapse stop doing all the things that help maintain sobriety. Then they become confused. Without healthy influence, they begin to wonder just how bad the problem really was, doubting they were truly addicted. Next they begin to compromise, going to unhealthy places and setting themselves up for failure. Then finally the catastrophe occurs. They return to drinking and drugging. The entire recovery process is stopped, and everyone must begin again.

These four stages of relapse are a predictable progression as easily recognized as the initial progression toward addiction. And at any point the progression can stop with the proper intervention. All a parent must do is recognize that recovery has been sidetracked and relapse is in the making. The following are ten indicators that a young addict is moving away from recovery and into relapse:

1. Negative relationships. The child begins dating or hanging around with kids known for their heavy drinking and drug-taking.

This will probably be rationalized as an attempt to help them, but that's just a coverup for the desire to return to negative behavior.

2. Dishonesty. He or she starts to lie and is caught in those lies. Even lies about insignificant things are a warning that your child is being dishonest in other areas, such as chemical abuse.

3. A critical spirit. Your child begins to move out of gratitude and into repeated criticism. This is often a process of projection as a way of coping with the guilt from irresponsible behavior. Confront the critical comments as soon as you notice them.

4. Self-centeredness. This coincides with the critical and ungrateful attitude. When selfishness is evidenced, spiritual and emotional recovery have been hampered.

5. Isolation. He or she begins to separate from the family and becomes unwilling to participate in family activities.

6. Low frustration tolerance. The child appears to be less able to cope with the minor irritations of life, becoming easily frustrated.

7. Anxiety. He or she grows more anxious. Serenity disappears.

8. Defiance. Rebellious rage begins to replace love and acceptance.

9. Grandiosity. This closely parallels dishonesty. The addict starts to have unrealistic plans, and his conversations are quite removed from reality.

10. Depression. He or she is depressed and constantly in a bad mood, spending many hours sleeping.

When the above signals begin to surface, your child has become complacent in the recovery plan. The sooner you intervene, the greater the chance to avoid the catastrophe of a relapse.

Ten Threats to Recovery

Knowing the symptoms of relapse doesn't mean you should sit back and wait for them to appear. Instead, work together with your children to identify and avoid the main threats to recovery. These are the things that usually trip up recovering people. Learn about these, and discuss them with your kids. And when you see them succumbing to one or more, warn them and help them to stay on course. The ten threats are:

1. Guilt. Irresponsible behavior such as dishonesty will produce guilt. Many people drink and abuse drugs in response to unresolved guilt. Responsible behavior is the best way to avoid the problem.

2. Unhealthy relationships. Kids don't stay sober with drunk friends.

3. Holidays. Reality rarely matches our high expectations of the holidays. Tension is often created in bringing multiple generations together. Parties and advertisements also encourage drinking. These are tough times, and everyone needs to give extra support to recovering addicts.

4. Hunger. Blood sugar levels drop and emotions are on edge in the wake of hunger. A person in recovery should not go too long without eating.

5. High pressure situations. The anticipation of high pressure situations and the letdown when they're over send anxiety levels soaring. Before or after these kinds of situations, a recovering person must be aware that feelings are often out of control. He or she needs to learn to wait for anxiety to level out rather than act on impulse to relieve the tension through chemicals.

6. Anger. When resentment builds into anger, danger is at hand. Millions of relapses have happened when a person was angry at someone else.

7. Lack of sleep. Tired and irritable people lose control and relapse.

8. Loneliness. Strong recovery must involve remaining connected to people both socially and emotionally. Make plans to prevent extended periods of loneliness.

9. Self-pity. In aftercare and recovery groups, people have to be reminded not to indulge in pity parties. Feeling sorry for yourself often leads to feeling you deserve a drink or drug. The opposite of self-pity is gratitude. Grateful people do not return to alcohol or drugs.

10. Overconfidence. People relapse because they think they're the exception to the rule. They believe they don't need to go to meetings or hear lectures. They even think they can be around other people who drink or do drugs. Some even tend bar while others drink. Those are acts of overconfidence, and they always spell trouble.

These ten threats can be countered. But people in recovery are often blind to their reality, so they need to be confronted by a concerned person. Your child may not want to listen to your suggestions, however, due to unresolved resentment or some other reason.

Thus, it's important that early in the recovery process your child find a sponsor—another recovering person who can hold him or her accountable for meeting attendance, assignment completion, and staying clean. A sponsor must not be afraid to confront your child with the reality of the situation. He or she must know the threats to recovery and discuss them with your child. The sponsor understands the cravings and struggles and is there for your child to call, day or night, when facing the temptation to relapse. He or she also provides a model of successful recovery.

Conclusion

Relapse isn't just one incidence of out-of-control behavior. It isn't just the return to drugs and alcohol. It's a shift in attitude and actions that starts a predictable, downhill progression. That progression can be interrupted and recovery salvaged before it's too late. But to intervene, you must be actively involved with your child's recovery. Attend meetings, read recovery materials, and find a support group for yourself. Being active requires sacrifice, but that sacrifice is minimal compared to the pain of watching kids bounce in and out of treatment centers. Your children need you in the recovery process. Your love and assistance are the most powerful protections against relapse.

If relapse does occur, it's not the end of the world or the end of recovery. If handled well, it can be the beginning of long-term sobriety. Often kids need to press the limits to determine where the line exists between freedom to act and the need to preserve sobriety. Discovering the limitations may be all it takes to turn them toward a process of total recovery. Remember that many people who have a heart attack have relapses. All sorts of problems subject the person to relapse. Don't lose hope or give up. Instead, forgive and move quickly to return adolescents to the recovery process. Your children need you more than ever.

Jerry ended treatment for drug addiction at age sixteen. The day he left the treatment center to go back into the big, bad world, he relapsed. On his seventeenth birthday, he entered a stricter program. He didn't last two weeks before he was back out, partying as if he had never been to treatment.

Jerry's parents hurt deeply. They wanted to protect him from more harm, but they also knew true love must be tough. So they stuck to his recovery plan, which said, "If Jerry goes back into a substance abuse lifestyle, we (his parents) will not welcome him back in our home unless he will re-enter a treatment facility."

After six tries in and out of treatment, he crawled back to his parents and said, "This time it will work." Today Jerry is a certified drug- and alcohol-treatment-center counselor, making a difference in the lives of other recovering addicts. His parents' choice to administer a tough kind of love and stick to the recovery plan saved him.

CHAPTER TWELVE

Motivating Others to Drug-Proof Their Kids

In Albuquerque, New Mexico, a group of parents have banded together to curb drug abuse and provide treatment for kids who need help. Their organization is called Parents Against Drugs, and they have approached the city with an innovative idea. When a child is caught with drugs or alcohol at school, he or she would be transferred to another school where everyone enrolled is dealing with the same struggle. The students would provide tremendous support for each other to stay drug-free. This would give access to a treatment program to many kids who normally would not be able to receive quality help. It would also be much less expensive than most treatment facilities.

These parents may not succeed in getting the school established. But they have obtained the ear of the community and its officials.

In Fort Worth, Texas, various sectors of the community are pulling together to do something about drunk driving. From businesses, parents, PTAs, and anonymous groups, there's a cooperative effort to reduce drunk driving deaths on New Year's Eve. Free rides home are provided to those who become drunk.

In Philadelphia, parents became angry watching the crack dealers move into the heart of their neighborhoods. They refused to sit back and be taken over by drug pushers, and as a result, their group is one of the best-informed in the country about drugs. Law enforcement agencies trained the parents how to observe behavior the way police do, identifying actions consistent with drug pushing and dealing. Now, as trained observers, they have credibility when they call the police with a complaint about a drug dealer on the street.

Because these parents learned how to spot the problem and took action when they did, they have totally cleaned up some neighborhoods that were infested with crack and its dealers. When parents decide to do something, they can have a tremendous impact on a community.

If you've been frustrated with the lack of progress in your community regarding drug and alcohol abuse, you're not alone. Thousands of parents across the country have grown disgusted as they've watched their communities deteriorate and their children be destroyed. Many of those parents have banded together to form groups like those in Albuquerque and Philadelphia. They stopped expecting someone else to solve the problem and decided to do something themselves. We believe it's time that parents stop pointing fingers and start looking for ways that everyone in a community can help stop chemical abuse. In this chapter we want to suggest ways that you, along with others, can take effective action.

Parent Power

When parents pull together to save their kids and protect their community, they often succeed, as illustrated by the preceding examples. But such efforts must start with someone. One concerned parent has to be willing to take the initiative for drug-free kids. In every case where a community has turned around its drug problem, the process began with one person who decided to rally the other parents. You can be that person. You can be responsible for changing the lives of thousands of young people and saving a community.

One of the best ways to motivate others is to form a community advisory board. The purpose of such a board is to inform and educate people of the hazards of drug and alcohol abuse and to act on the information. One board in New Jersey put together flyers giving parents discussion-starter questions to use in talking with their children. They organized a telephone hotline and parent seminars, and they chaperoned school dances.

You can start a board just by asking people to serve, or you can join an existing organization. We suggest you call a reporter and ask for a story announcing the first meeting in the local newspaper. An advisory board should include prominent members of the community: physicians, nurses, and others from the medical community; educators and leaders in parent-teacher groups; pastors and church youth workers; professionals from the treatment field who understand addiction; and leaders from civic groups, such as Rotary and Kiwanis. Perhaps the most important contributors are the parents in the community, who should be invited to come and express their concerns before the group.

Many communities have an active city council that's willing to listen to people. In such cases, rather than form an advisory board, you might choose to organize parents to lobby the city council, asking it to pass helpful laws or fund treatment programs. This approach might require going door-to-door to ask parents to come to a meeting, but if they will come in large enough numbers, most city officials will be accommodating. Forming an advisory board or organizing parents to approach the city council can be the first important step in a grass-roots effort to change the direction of the drug problem.

Parents can take many other steps. One of the most effective is to insure that existing laws are strictly enforced in the community. Police frequently complain that it does no good to arrest people if the judge is going to put them back on the street. Mothers Against Drunk Driving did a wonderful thing when they began to monitor judges who sentenced people convicted of driving under the influence of alcohol. Because of their efforts, progress is being made against drunk driving for the first time in our nation's history.

Your group may likewise want to approach a judge or two about their leniency and how that affects your children. Encourage strict enforcement of the laws forbidding drug dealing, using, and drinking by minors.

School systems are ripe for innovative programs. Every time a school system organizes to attack the problem, many lives are diverted from the path of addiction. Parents can volunteer to form intervention groups in the school. If children are caught with alcohol or drugs, they can be referred to a committee that assesses the problem and recommends or demands action. The committee can send kids to counseling, treatment centers, or special courses on alcohol and drugs, or it can insist that they be separated from other kids. Many schools have set up such committees composed of parents, teachers, and school administrators.

In 1986, I (Jim) was asked to speak at a public high school assembly in Whittier, California, on "Making Decisions About Drugs and Alcohol." The assembly was sponsored by the school's PTA, and the program was well received. The leader of the PTA even told me ahead of time that I was free to mention my belief that people can have a personal relationship with Jesus Christ and that He cares about the chemically addicted.

After the assembly, I asked this wonderful woman how she got involved in putting on these programs. She told me that she had gone to her first PTA meeting the previous year. The group was a little apathetic. They had $8,000 budgeted for "prevention" assemblies, but no one wanted to invest the time needed to organize them, so no assemblies had been planned.

That night after the meeting, she couldn't sleep. It bothered her that this group had the opportunity to influence kids in a positive way but didn't have the energy. The next day she volunteered to be in charge of the assemblies. In the first year, she brought in programs on drugs and alcohol, setting standards, sexual abuse, peer pressure, and crisis pregnancy. The students loved the new approach, and after each assembly the speaker would invite kids to another room to talk. I met with more than fifty students who wanted to talk about their drug and alcohol problems the day I spoke. My friend's decision to invest her time in the PTA was richly rewarded.

Doug Fields and Jim Hancock are two church youth workers who volunteer to sit on drug abuse committees. They have had numerous opportunities to make presentations to junior high and high school students simply because they volunteered.

When money is available, parents can motivate their cities to do some very creative and helpful things. New treatment centers can be built. With treatment beds available, the courts can use alternative sentencing programs. Rather than sending kids to jail on a first offense, judges can mandate them into treatment programs. Innovative prevention programs can be set up in schools, along with procedures for intervention at the first sign of a problem.

Just as parental prevention revolves around increasing rewards or restrictions based on children's conduct, so can school-based prevention programs. One reward is scholarship money. A fund could be established for those children who go through school and have no record of a drug or alcohol violation and who swear, with five supporting statements from others, that they have not used drugs or alcohol. This is expensive and extreme, but it could motivate some kids not to use.

The restriction side of the prevention program must have some severe penalties. Judges must be willing to restrict freedom and privilege. If they are, many kids will be deterred from becoming involved. Parents should also work to get state laws changed so that any minor caught driving while intoxicated or on drugs, or selling drugs from a car would automatically have his or her driver's license suspended for one year. That's a very effective restriction with adolescents. They may not be able to sense the reality of prison, but they can feel the impact of going a year without being able to drive.

Parents can also band together to hold each other accountable to uphold the laws. First they must agree that alcohol and drugs are unacceptable at all school functions and community parties for teenagers. Any function that includes drinking and drugging should be shut down, and those responsible should be arrested. Parents also need to agree to let the offenders stay in jail, not bailing them out instantly.

But, more important, parents need to agree that any parent supplying or allowing kids access to alcohol will be turned in and prosecuted for contributing to the delinquency of a minor. Too many efforts of concerned parents are sabotaged by other parents who don't understand the dangers of alcohol and drugs. Don't let such a parent get away with harming your children. We've seen too many lives ruined because someone did not want to offend another adult.

Parents who have the potential to harm your kids can be helped in a support group. Such a group will provide guidance to those who struggle with kids using drugs. It offers a place where they can ask questions of other parents about drug prevention or some problem that has come up in the family. The support group can also encourage people who don't have children with a drug problem but just need a place to pour out their discouragement in the fight against chemical abuse.

You don't have to be a counselor or psychologist to run a support group. Just put up a notice and tell people the purpose of the group. When the first person comes, you have begun a support group that could be the nucleus for the drug-proof movement and a major source of parent power.

Positive Peer Power

Before you motivate the parents to band together, you may want to get the kids together. When children become involved in positive peer influence groups, it's usually easy to motivate their parents to help the community fight drugs and alcohol. When peer groups of this nature form, they are based on a pledge by all the members, to each other and to their parents, to remain drug-free.

For many who live in the inner city, this might sound naive. It's not. Many kids want to belong to something worthwhile and meaningful. They join a gang or a drug-using group of friends because of a lack of alternatives. Thus, a group of positive peer support could be the key to a drug-free life. We are encouraged by the numerous S.A.D.D. (Students Against Drunk Driving) groups in schools across the country.

In Jackson, Mississippi, kids have banded together under the leadership of their parents. They have formed a patrol group to go through the town and look for suspicious behavior. When they see what appears to be a drug deal, they phone the police, who respond immediately. Working with the police in this way develops respect for law enforcement and understanding of the men and women in uniform. It gives the children a sense of importance and accomplishment. It's a "hobby" that takes up time productively. For many, it's the alternative they need to stay off drugs. It also brings parents together to help the kids and motivates parents to clean up their own lives.

Another positive peer association for kids comes through drama. In one town, kids volunteered to perform plays about drug and alcohol abuse. In studying and acting out the parts, they came to understand more fully the feelings and consequences surrounding drug abuse. Some of the kids were former drug users, and the plays helped them understand their own problems and maintain sobriety. The plays were done all over the community, and hundreds of people were motivated to get involved in some manner of drug and alcohol prevention.

Whether it be drama or other activities, bring the kids in your community together in new and exciting ways. Provide them with the alternatives they need. And ask their parents to join you in your fight.

The Church in Action

When the war against drugs is won, it will be because all the community has come together to help. We both have seen churches as an effective part of such efforts. This is not a task to be left to the youth workers or Sunday school teachers; it's a project for the entire church. The first step in motivating a church to respond is to train the staff, elected leaders, and teachers in the areas of drug education, prevention, and treatment. When a common base of knowledge is developed, the church leadership can respond in unity to help the community.

Once the staff has been educated, courses should be offered for parents. They need to know the facts and prevention concepts so they can relay them to their kids and support the action of the church. When the parents have been made knowledgeable, it's time to educate the kids. Children are not educated best by lectures. Bring in a recovering addict to tell his or her story. Show films that present the realities of drug abuse in graphic form. Have other kids who have overcome the problem talk about recovery. Educate the children of your church with as much exposure to the subject as possible. Be creative in designing new ways to present the information.

If you know the drug-prevention resources in your community, the job of lining up good presentations will be much easier. The Yellow Pages or the local Council on Alcoholism are good places to start looking. Work with the prevention and treatment groups on educating kids and counseling those with problems. Even if these groups aren't run by people with strong Christian principles, they possess important information and experience. In the process of working with you, they will see the church apart from the caricatures developed by the media.

One of the most helpful things a church can do is organize parents to provide healthy activities when adolescent temptations are at a peak. Give the kids pizza parties after games and dances. A game night can be fun for everyone. The times when teens are most likely to get into trouble are the times when the church's creative resources can be most beneficial. Don't be afraid to work with other churches on these projects, either. Pooled resources can make it possible to provide a greater variety of positive and fun alternatives. The church can set the standard of leadership for the rest of the community.

Taking the Twelve Steps to Church

Some Christians are skeptical of the twelve-step programs because they aren't usually affiliated with a church. However, we're excited about the large number of churches now sponsoring Alcoholics Anonymous programs as part of their ministry.

We believe the twelve steps are very much in line with the Bible. Unfortunately, throughout the years people have largely lost the true meaning of who the "higher power" is. Dr. Vernon J. Bittner has revised the twelve steps for Christians. His desire was to reclaim the twelve steps for the church and to be specific about the identity of our "Higher Power."

Here are what Bittner calls the twelve steps for Christian living:

1. We admit our need for God's gift of salvation, confessing we are powerless over certain areas of our lives and that our lives are at times sinful and unmanageable.

2. We come to believe through the Holy Spirit that a power who came in the person of Jesus Christ and who is greater than ourselves can transform our weaknesses into strengths.

3. We make a decision to turn our wills and our lives over to the care of Jesus Christ as we understand Him, hoping to understand Him more fully.

4. We make a searching and fearless moral inventory of ourselves, both our strengths and our weaknesses.

5. We admit to Christ, to ourselves, and to another human being the exact nature of our sins.

6. We become entirely ready to have Christ heal all those defects of character that prevent us from having a more spiritual lifestyle.

7. We humbly ask Christ to transform all our shortcomings.

8. We make a list of all persons we have harmed and become willing to make amends to them all.

9. We make direct amends to such persons whenever possible, except when to do so would injure them or others.

10. We continue to take personal inventory, and when we're wrong, we promptly admit it. When we're right, we thank God for His guidance.

11. We seek through prayer and meditation to improve our conscious contact with Jesus Christ, as we understand Him,

praying for knowledge of God's will for us and the power to carry that out.

12. Having experienced a new sense of spirituality as a result of these steps, and realizing this is a gift of God's grace, we are willing to share the message of Christ's love and forgiveness with others and to practice these principles for spiritual living in all our affairs.[1]

Anyone can start a movement. There's no reason the person in your community who makes the biggest difference can't be you. Your action can mobilize the forces of the press, the school system, law enforcement, and parents to defeat the drug problem in your town. The drug war cannot be won alone. It requires the help of every area of the community. But one person with compassion and commitment can motivate others to begin the fight.

One housewife has made a big difference in our community. Molly Frye is the mother of three teenagers. A few years ago, she got fed up with what her kids were being taught about sex and drug abuse in the school system, and she decided to do something about it.

Without a day's experience in formal youth work, Molly wrote a curriculum for both crisis pregnancy and drug and alcohol abuse. As a guest instructor, she presented her curriculum in a health class. It was so well received that last year she and a modest band of volunteers spoke to more than 16,000 students in our community. One person can make a difference.

CHAPTER THIRTEEN

It's Never too Late to Begin

Robert was a computer genius by the age of fourteen. He was introduced to computers at twelve, and within two years he was writing his own programs. At sixteen, one of his games was picked up and distributed by a major software publisher. Within three years, the royalties had made him wealthy.

But even with his sky-high I.Q., Robert wasn't smart enough to stay away from drugs. In his hours-long programming marathons, he used cocaine to fuel his creativity. When he was done, he smoked marijuana to relax and come down. It didn't take long for both his money and his drive to disappear. At age twenty-five, he was penniless, homeless, and living on the streets of Phoenix.

His parents put him in drug and alcohol treatment centers and psychiatric hospitals and even sent him on a missionary work cruise. Nothing helped. The court system jailed Robert a number of times and finally gave up on him. The judge took him off probation and told him and his parents there was nothing more he could do. Robert would have to change or face a long prison sentence. He returned to the streets to do odd jobs, make a few dollars, and buy marijuana. Drugs always took precedence over food.

At age twenty-eight, suffering from malnutrition and pneumonia, Robert was admitted to Phoenix General Hospital. He wanted to die, and his parents expected he would. His physicians talked to him about his lack of will to live. They did everything they could to help, but nothing seemed to work, and Robert weakened steadily.

When hope was but a thread, a divine intervention took place. A newly hired nurse took care of Robert one evening. She helped him bathe and perform his bodily functions. And as she helped him physically, she also ministered to him spiritually. She told her own story of addiction, despair, and recovery. She talked of a loving God who had helped her find new meaning in life. She spent hours telling Robert he was not alone, he was loved, and she cared.

Somehow her words crept into Robert's empty heart and filled him with a new desire to live. In his weakness, he turned to God for strength and guidance to begin again. The subsequent process of recovery took him into drug treatment and hundreds of Alcoholics Anonymous meetings. From the brink of death was born a new life that has helped others find new hope as well. He has taken his simple message to anyone who will listen: "It's never too late to change."

The time to move into action is now. Whether you have young children or you have a fifty-year-old "child," it is never too late to start helping with a drug or alcohol problem. If your children have already succumbed to substance abuse, it's easy to think there's no hope.

Out of remorse, you may spend your time dwelling on the "if onlys." You say to yourself, "If only I had protected my child from the beginning." Keeping your focus on the "if onlys" or the "what ifs," however, only delays needed action. Rather than think of where you went wrong or where you could have done better, begin where you are. For years you may have rationalized that there was nothing you could do. Now you know that through intervention you may be able to change the course of your child's future. It will take great courage for you to act. And since there are no magical cures, it will take perseverance to alter the behavior that may have existed for years.

The alternative to acting, however, is to do nothing, a choice full of misery for yourself and those you could help. It's painful to intervene in a person's life, but the pain of intervention is much less than that of watching an alcohol or drug problem lead to death or insanity. Many parents sit back and pray that something will happen to help their children. They wait for a miraculous intervention that will stop the addiction quickly and painlessly. While they sit back, however, perhaps God is calling them to move into action. Maybe He's calling you to move into action to save your own children or the children of someone in your neighborhood.

You may not have children who are into drugs. Your kids may just be starting kindergarten or the first grade. You look into a pair of sweet, innocent eyes, and you question whether you should trouble this precious person with the worries of drug and alcohol abuse. It's hard to believe your children could be approached with a drug at so young an age. But for the sake of your kids and your community, please believe us: it's never too early.

Take the information you now have and discuss it with your children at age four or five. Teach them how to say no when approached with magic pills or the promise that they'll feel as if they're living in a fairy tale. Show them what harmful substances look like, and warn them of the actions and motives of those who would offer such substances to them.

Parents of addicted kids don't act for several reasons. Some think they can handle the problem alone. They can't. Others delay because they don't want to accept the finality of a diagnosis of drug addiction or alcoholism. Anything but one of those labels for their children! So they rely on home remedies that always fail, or they resort to quick fixes that only put a Band-Aid on a severe wound. Others wait in the hope that the child is going through a phase. But the "phase" will not go away. It's locked in by the addiction process. Until the parents act, it will not get any better.

Often parents delay action because they realize they may have to face problems of their own that they have worked hard to hide. Because of scars from the past or a marriage gone sour, they become so wrapped up in their own misery that they have little time to help a child prevent potential problems. They become so numbed by their own pain that they begin to believe their children must also suffer. The focus remains on the parents' problems. Parents must find a way to work through their difficulties and free themselves to help their children. If they don't, the struggles and pain are passed from generation to generation.

A man had a son who was an adolescent alcoholic and a daughter who was a cocaine addict. This father spent about a year in constant worry over their problems. At the end of the day, he would leave the stress of his work to return home, where the stress and pain were even greater. His normal glass of wine with dinner became a mixed drink before dinner, many glasses of wine during dinner, and drinks afterward. His tolerance was as large as his son's. It wasn't until he took his son to an A.A. meeting that he discovered that what was in his son was also in himself. He then started recovery alongside his son. The whole family joined in recovery because the father faced his own problem.

That example, unfortunately, is the exception. Most parents refuse to face their problems and addictions. They thereby fail themselves and their children. It takes courage to be the exception rather than the rule.

You may have turned to alcohol or drugs because of the pain in your own life. Or like many others, you may have been developing an addiction problem for years without knowing it. You may have come to rely on prescription drugs to help you get by. And in the midst of your struggle, you look at your children and hope they'll have a better life. You want to help them stay off alcohol and drugs. But you can't help kids stay off alcohol and drugs if you're using sleeping pills every night or you're a practicing alcoholic. The strongest message your children hear from you is the message they see. If you have a drug or alcohol problem, we urge you to take care of it as soon as possible.

You may be a heavy drinker and yet not be convinced you have a problem. Your reluctance to help your children might be subconscious because of doubts about yourself.

Knowing for Sure You Have a Problem

This whole subject may produce repeated cringes from the guilt you feel about your own drinking. As many recovering alcoholics know, the times of greatest guilt are the times of highest motivation to stop drinking. They might come after a binge or after bailing a child out of jail for driving while intoxicated. You might have done something that humiliated the family and shattered the image of a family "with its act together." Perhaps reading this book or experiencing one of those dreadful moments has led you to question whether you have a problem severe enough that it demands you quit drinking. Or perhaps you've been dabbling in drugs, and you want to know if you've become addicted. The following points will help you determine if in fact you have an alcohol or drug problem.

1. High tolerance. As we've mentioned before, alcoholics and drug addicts all have one thing in common: the ability to drink or drug a lot.

The large amount of chemical addicts the body to the point where the cells crave it. What is a large amount is different for each individual, but you know if you're one of those who can drink or drug more than others. You've probably passed on to your kids the ability to consume vast quantities of an addictive chemical, making them sitting ducks for the same problem.

Growing up in Texas, I (Steve) was around many people who took great pride in their ability to hold liquor. It wasn't uncommon to be at social functions and watch the men consume beer after beer all day and into the night. These were not drunkards or irresponsible men. But they had been brought up with the understanding that manhood had something to do with the ability to hold alcohol and maintain control. These people drank this way for most of their lives and produced children who drank that way also.

It wasn't until later in life, because of aging, that their tolerance went down. When their bodies could no longer process the alcohol, their drinking became unpredictable and uncontrollable. Then they were recognized as having a drinking problem. But my Texan friends were alcoholic long before their livers quit working or their drinking went out of control.

If you have a high tolerance for drugs or alcohol, you need to get help. You have become addicted, and that addiction will not go away. It will begin to control you in more painful and obvious ways. The only way to control it is through abstinence.

2. Compulsion to use again and again. The person with an alcohol or drug problem will consume large amounts and do it over and over. Between times of using, the compulsion to use again controls all thoughts and emotions. The person is obsessed with when and where the next drink or drug will be taken. Without the alcohol or drug in the system, the addict feels incomplete and needs the chemical either to feel better or just to feel normal.

Some addicts go for months without using a drug or taking a drink and by going that long think they're in control. But during those times of restraint, they continually think about what it would be like to drink or use. They "white knuckle" it, hanging on to anything they can that will prevent drug use that day. That can hardly be called "being in control." In fact, the chemical has total control. The compulsion lives and grows inside. Finally, it drives them to repeat the act of drinking and using.

3. Intense dysphoria. Euphoria is the feeling of intense pleasure. The opposite is dysphoria. People drink or take drugs in search of euphoria. When most people stop, they return to a normal state. But if you're an addict, there is no return to normal. If you stop consuming, you experience intense dysphoria.

You feel intense agony and depression. You have tremendous, uncontrollable mood swings. Thoughts and emotions are extremely hard to bear. You may cry uncontrollably. You may even have attempted suicide in times of dark struggle. You feel this way because your nerves are accustomed to the chemical, and without its saturation, your entire psychological economy is distorted. You become emotionally bankrupt. You desperately return to the chemical to ease the pain.

Dysphoria and its consequences have been more fully understood since the crack epidemic swept across our country. This chemical gives an intense high followed by a screeching dysphoria that thrusts the user into deep despair. The user is left craving the drug in an effort to stop the emotional pain. If you feel worse when you stop using than you did when you started, your body is addicted. We don't know anyone who can honestly say, "My life is better because of my use of illegal drugs."

4. Continued use in the midst of adverse circumstances. It isn't normal to watch problems increase all around you and still continue the behavior that causes them. Family, friends, job, self-esteem, and many other good things will be destroyed as you continue to hang on to something that can no longer bring you satisfaction. The only reason you continue is that the addiction has you hooked. You wouldn't make a rational decision to destroy your life for the sake of a chemical. But because you're trapped in addiction, you continue to use no matter how bad your life becomes.

When people are addicted, the consequences begin to affect certain areas of life. But soon they affect every area. For each person the order may be different, but the adverse consequences are inevitable. Family problems erupt as the drinking and drugging drive family members away, each one feeling betrayed and hurt. Job performance declines. Friends go the other way, repulsed by actions the addict takes under the influence. The irritating effects of the chemicals wear down the body and cause disease. But as tragedy after tragedy mounts up, the addict still refuses to make a move toward recovery. This failure occurs not because the person is weak but because of the powerful grip that addiction has on the body.

5. *Other people telling you there's a problem.* The strongest indicator of addiction is that others have taken the risk of telling you you're not normal. They have not done that to hurt you, and they certainly haven't done it hastily. They have put it off many times and finally could put it off no longer. And when you hear it from more than one person, don't think there's a conspiracy. Believe that others care enough to confront you. You have a problem, and you must get help.

There's an old saying that if one person calls you a horse, ignore it. If two people call you a horse, ask what they mean. But if three people call you a horse, it's time to saddle up. If these indicators are in your life, it's time for you to saddle up to the responsibility of doing something about them. It's time to get help so you can help your children avoid the pain and suffering you've experienced.

If these indicators make you uncomfortable, it's because you can too easily relate to them. Wait no longer. Recovery won't kill you. The drugs and alcohol will. Make a decision for your own good and contact a professional or call the number in the back of this book.

The above may not describe you and your feelings, but it might describe your spouse. If you live with an alcoholic or drug addict, you have seen those symptoms develop over the years. Take what you've learned from the chapter on intervention and apply it to your spouse. One of the reasons your children have chosen the way of drugs is that you haven't stopped the progression in your mate. As a result, the kids have modeled the behavior they've seen or used chemicals to escape the pain of the family. Don't wait any longer.

The greatest gift you can give your family is the willingness to struggle through the pain of intervention. When you do, it can be the beginning of a new family and a new life. It's never too late to start.

Drug-proof kids come from drug-free parents. Free yourself and your family. Become willing to do whatever it takes to raise drug-proof children in a drug-saturated society. Life comes with no guarantees, but your actions are the best hope for saving your children from the destruction of alcohol and drugs.

Summary for Drug-Proofing

1. Education: Teach your children the facts about alcohol and drug abuse. Ensure that they know the consequences.
2. Prevention: Use both positive and negative reinforcements to motivate your child to make the decision to abstain.
3. Identification: Learn to identify the signs of drug and alcohol use and abuse. If your child uses, be the first to know.
4. Intervention: If you discover your child has a problem, act now to intervene. Seek help rather than expect the problem to go away.
5. Treatment: Find the resources that best fit your situation and

uphold the values of your faith and family.

6. Supportive Follow-up: Prevent relapse by becoming an active participant in your child's recovery.
7. Self-Evaluation: Examine your own involvement with alcohol and drugs. Solve your problem before you try to help your child.

If you or your child need information on obtaining help for an alcohol or drug problem, call 1-800-227-LIFE.

Drug-proof your kids material is also available in video and audio formats. These tapes are excellent for churches and schools. For information, contact:

Outreach Ministries
570 Glenneyre, Suite 107
Laguna Beach, CA 92651
714-494-7806

Appendix

One way to enhance kids' ability to withstand pressure is through playing the game that follows. Used in your family or with a youth group, it teaches refusal techniques. Its best use is between a parent and a child, going over each pressure situation and talking it through.

The "Just Say No" Game

The object of the game is to respond to a high-pressure situation in such a way that those applying pressure will back off. Try to come up with several creative ways to say no.

Drug Offers

1. You are at school in between classes, and someone asks you to walk into the bathroom to smoke a joint.

2. A boy you know says he snuck two of his mother's tranquilizers out of the medicine cabinet and asks you to meet him after school to take them.

3. One of the high school seniors offers to give you a ride home and tells you he has some crack that is pure and expensive.

4. At one of the local hangouts, a girl offers you a red pill and promises it will make you feel as though you are in another world.

5. You see a friend under the football stadium, shooting something in his arm. He offers to let you try it for free.

6. On the way to the show, someone in the car pulls out a handful of pills for everyone to try. He insists that all participate.

7. Your date lights up a joint.

8. At a slumber party, one of the kids starts handing out sleeping pills from her parents' medicine cabinet.

9. You open your notebook in class and find a small envelope with a red pill in it. You look up, and a boy you know is winking at you. He takes a pill like the one you have and puts it in his mouth.

10. Before a basketball game, one of the guys on the team says he has a pill to give everyone super energy so that the team can win.

11. On the way home from a movie, while stopped at a traffic light, someone comes to the car window and offers you some crack for ten dollars.

12. At a party, a girl pulls out of her purse a mirror and a vial of cocaine. The entire party watches you, the first person to be offered the white powder.

13. A guy you know is walking with you to see a friend. He pulls from his pocket a cigarette that he says is dusted with PCP. He says that the one he smoked yesterday was wonderful.

14. A girl at a party goes into the kitchen to bake some brownies. The rumor circulates that one of the ingredients is marijuana. She offers you the first sample.

Alcohol Offers

1. Your older brother and his friend pick you up from a party, and his friend offers you a cold beer for the trip home.

2. At a party, the gang gets into the parents' liquor cabinet. Everyone starts drinking out of the bottle of vodka.

3. Your parents take you out to a nice dinner at a local club. Your dad orders everyone something to drink and tells you it's okay for you to have one.

4. On the drive home from school, one of the people you considered to be your friend pulls out a bottle of champagne and pops the cork, asking you to drink up.

5. On a fishing trip, you go up the river with your brother. You are in the middle of the forest, and he says that since no one is around you can have a beer.

6. There is a secret club, and you want to get in. At the initiation ceremony, the leader hands you a quart bottle of beer and tells you that to be part of the club, you must drink it.

7. Your friend's dad is offering all of the kids at the party a beer to loosen up.

8. At a local restaurant, by mistake the waiter pours you a glass of wine.

9. Behind a shed in the vacant lot near your house, you and a friend find a six-pack of beer that is still cold. Your friend suggests the two of you drink it all.

10. You are on a trip to Hawaii, and the stewardess offers you some rum punch like all the other passengers are drinking.

11. At church camp, one of the counselors, who seems to like you, asks you to meet him outside the bunk house when lights go out. You go, thinking it will be a special project or a joke on someone. When you get there, you see that he has a bottle in his hand, and he smells like he has been drinking. He asks you if you would like some.

12. You get invited to a party of older kids. You are told that everyone will be there, including a celebrity from Hollywood. The person inviting you tells you that everyone will be drinking and asks you to come along.

13. On the way home from school, your friend's father begins to drink while he is driving.

14. On a ski trip to the lake, your older cousin takes you out in the boat to the middle of the lake. When you get there, he opens a silver flask full of bourbon and says to take a drink, it won't hurt you.

15. At a local club, to get beer you need to have a stamp on your hand. A friend of yours tells you to meet him at seven o'clock in front of the club. He says he can get your hand stamped so you can get beer.

16. At a Sunday brunch, the waiter pours everyone some champagne, including you. Your sister looks at you and says to take a drink, it comes with the price of the food.

Notes

Chapter 1: Drugs at Your Doorstep

1. Barbara R. Lorch and Robert H. Hughes, "Church Youth, Alcohol and Drug Education Programs and Youth Substance Use," *Journal of Alcohol and Drug Education*, vol. 33, no. 2 (Winter 1988): 15.
2. "Alcohol Use and Abuse in America," *The Gallup Report*, no. 265 (October 1987): 3.
3. Ibid.
4. Ibid., 15.

Chapter 2: Just How Bad Is It?

1. Tom Parker, *In One Day: The Things Americans Do in a Day* (Boston: Houghton Mifflin Co., 1984), 31.
2. *Facts on Alcoholism and Alcohol-Related Problems* (New York: National Council on Alcoholism, 1988), 6.
3. Ibid.
4. Edward W. Desmond, "Out in the Open," *Time*, 30 November 1987, 90.
5. "Coming to Grips with Alcoholism," *U.S. News & World Report*, 30 November 1987, 56.
6. "Alcohol Use and Abuse in America," *The Gallup Report*, no. 265 (October 1987): 44.
7. Jerry Adler, "Hour by Hour Crack," *Newsweek*, 28 November 1988, 67.
8. Ibid., 66.
9. "Study: Drug emergencies soar; Many cases result from cocaine use," *USA Today*, 7 November 1988, 3A.
10. Ibid.
11. Ibid.
12. Adler, *Hour by*, 64.
13. Ibid.
14. Ibid., 65.
15. "The Bottom Line on Alcohol in Society," *Alcohol Research Information Service*, vol. 8, no. 4 (Winter 1988), 11.
16. Ibid.
17. Ibid.
18. "What Drugs Do and Don't Do to Teens," *U.S. News & World Report*, 1 August 1988, 8.

Chapter 3: Road Blocks and Building Blocks

1. "Report to the People," Youth for Christ, December 1985.

2. Ken Barun and Philip Bashe, *How to Keep the Children You Love Off Drugs* (New York: Atlantic Monthly Press, 1988), 50.
3. "Under the Influence," (Pamphlet, National Federation of Parents for Drug-Free Youth, 1987), 4.
4. Bob Laird, "We're watching more TV," *USA Today*, 13 December 1988, 1D.
5. "Under the Influence," 8.
6. Barun and Bashe, *How to Keep*, 28.
7. Jim Burns, *The Youth Builder* (Eugene: Harvest House Publishers, Inc., 1988), 33-34.
8. *What Works: Schools Without Drugs* (Washington, D.C.: U. S. Department of Education, 1987), 15.
9. Donald W. Goodwin, M.D., *Is Alcoholism Hereditary?* (New York: Ballantine Books, Inc., 1988), 63.
10. Barun and Bashe, *How to Keep*, 4.
11. "Parents May Be Encouraging Kids to Smoke Pot," *Youth Worker Update* (September 1986), 3.
12. Ray Johnston, "Developing Leadership Potential in Students," El Cajon, Calif.: Youth Specialties, 1988. Sound cassette.
13. David Elkind, *The Hurried Child: Growing Up Too Fast Too Soon* (Reading: Addison-Wesley Publishing Co., Inc., 1981), 138.
14. H. Stephen Glenn, "Developing Capable Young People," El Cajon, Calif.: Youth Specialties, 1988. Sound cassette.

Chapter 4: Why Kids Take Drugs and Alcohol
1. Lorch and Hughes, "Church Youth, Alcohol," 15.
2. Ross Campbell, M.D., *Your Child and Drugs* (Wheaton: Victor Books, 1988), 70-71.
3. Ibid.
4. John Q. Baucom, Ph.D., *Help Your Children Say No to Drugs* (Grand Rapids: Zondervan Publishing House, 1987), 130-131.
5. H. Stephen Glenn and Jane Nelsen, *Raising Children for Success: Blueprints & Building Blocks for Developing Capable People* (Fair Oaks: Sunrise Press, 1987), 183.
6. Dennis Nelson, "Frequently seen stages in adolescent chemical use . . .," CompCare Publishers.
7. Baucom, *Help Your Children*, 34.
8. Ibid., 7.
9. Ibid., 57.

Chapter 5: Educating the Right Way at the Right Time
1. For a more detailed explanation of alcoholism, see *Growing Up Addicted*, Stephen Arterburn (Ballantine, 1987).

Chapter 7: Prevention Tools for Parents
1. Stephen Gibbons, et. al., "Patterns of Alcohol Use Among Rural and Small Towns," *Adolescence*, vol. 21 (1986): 893.
2. C. Kirk Hadway, Kirk W. Elifson, and David M. Peterson, "Religious Involvement and Drug Use Among Urban Adolescents," *Journal for the Scientific Study of Religion*, vol. 23 (1984): 109-128.

Chapter 8: Identifying Chemical Abuse in Your Kids
1. Jim Burns, *Youth Builder* (Eugene: Harvest House Publishers, Inc., 1988), 263-267.

Chapter 12: Motivating Others to Drug-Proof Their Kids
1. Vernon J. Bittner, "Twelve Steps for Christian Living," *Christianity Today*, 9 December 1988, 31.